The New Sun

The New Sun

With Archangel Michael

Mary Soliel

For Yia—
Thank you for being
a huge part of this book...
your beautiful gift of logo design,
lots of technical help, and always,
always, being there for me and steering
me on. ∞ love and cherish you, my
twin soul friend. ♡

Love,
Mare
and Michael
too!

TWELVE TWELVE PUBLISHING

Boulder, Colorado

The New Sun

With Archangel Michael

Twelve Twelve Publishing, LLC, books may be ordered through booksellers or Amazon.com.

Twelve Twelve Publishing, LLC
P.O. Box 822
Louisville, CO 80027 U.S.A.
www.twelvetwelvepublishing.com
alighthouse@mac.com

Logo Design: Lisa Kubik

Because of the dynamic nature of the Internet, any Web addresses or links contained in this book may have changed since publication and may no longer be valid.

ISBN: 978-0-9890169-3-3

This book
is dedicated to
all beings
behind
this greatest story
ever to be
told:

our new Heaven
on earth.

Contents

Acknowledgments

From my heart, my deepest gratitude goes to Archangel Michael, who, through his beautiful messages, graces us with the ability to understand, embrace, and persevere in our new lives. I am forever blessed by you, Michael. I call you, simply, Michael, because you are my friend. And I know you want us all to see you as our friend.

To the beautiful beings from the Heavenly realms who came through with their profound messages in the latter part of this book, I am very grateful. These messages rang so true in my heart, and they lift me up each time I reread them.

My heartfelt adoration and appreciation of my most loving supporters... my beautiful children, Scott and Karen, who cheer me on, relentlessly. With loving recognition of my dear parents who always display immense faith in me.

Special thanks to those whose presence had a measurable and blessed effect on this particular project: Lisa Kubik, my precious soul friend who generously offered her talents and support, and always kept me laughing; Clare Gippo, my kindred spirit and confidante who provided constant encouragement; Julie Libcke, my dear friend forevermore; Keith Doll, my caring spirit brother; Talia Horner, my darling daughter from another life; Angelita Loré and Miguel MacKenzie, mi sacrada familia; Cindy Winston, my sweet soul sister; Mia Mantello, who wrote a most touching song about Michael and me; Sue Elliott, my angel sent colleague; Mia Mantello, Margaret Rauenhorst, Cathy Kutchi, Loretta Pavlick, and Francine Donachie, for hosting me in their hometowns for presentations of Michael's messages; Jennifer Brocato and Jennifer Dioguardi, my soul sisters who beautifully support me in social media; and Leonard Duffy, Mia Milharycic, Kathy Galvan, Tina Hernandez, Ron Guthrie, Donna Stern, Joyce Hillman, Lee Ellis, and so many more beautiful souls, including those mentioned in my previous books, who have encouraged and inspired me in so many ways.

Preface

The title of this book, *The New Sun*, may sound a bit science fiction to you. As you know, our world is changing... and changing fast. Our lives are being turned upside down in the most absolutely positive way possible as we clear out the old—meaning the third dimensional aspects of our lives—and move into new and higher ways of being. So much is going on both inside and outside our very selves, on so many levels, preparing us for profound changes. And the New Sun is behind all that is occurring.

Everything that you will read about in this book, and that you, perhaps, also read in *Michael's Clarion Call: Messages from the Archangel for Creating Heaven on Earth*—specifically, the changes that we are currently experiencing and will continue to experience in the future—are only possible because of this new Light emanating from and through our sun. I invite you to read the following with an open and willing heart. By understanding and embracing the changes ahead, we will make our metamorphosis into a new kind of human on our new earth much easier, more graceful, and most exciting for us all.

Introduction

Let us talk about the sun. Something is indeed going on with our brilliant star, and, for most of us, it is without our conscious awareness. Yet, we seem to find ourselves naturally drawn to the sun, like never before. We wish to take pictures of it and its rays, or we simply desire to be outside and in the sunlight more often.

While it is easy to take the sun for granted, we also know that we simply would not be here, as human beings on this planet, if not for our sun. But our being more drawn to it isn't just out of a newer and suddenly growing appreciation of its gifts and grandness. It is because we sense that something is going on with our sun. We sense that something is changing.

In my book, *Michael's Clarion Call*, Archangel Michael talks about our channeling golden Liquid Light, through our developing Light bodies. He does not want this information to scare us, but rather to understand that if we are truly creating Heaven on our earth, should it not make sense that our bodies would be less dense, lighter, and more angel like? We have been receiving increasing amounts of this Light, which is, in large part, responsible for the physical and emotional symptoms that we are experiencing—commonly known as "Ascension Symptoms."

This Liquid Light is coming from what Michael refers to as the New Sun, also known as the Great Central Sun. It is not really new, but it is new to humans. The New Sun, our spiritual Sun, is coming through the sun we have known as 3rd dimensional beings, and this is exactly why we are experiencing changes with this sun that we are familiar with. While Liquid Light is not something we can see, at least not yet, we are *seeing* it through changes in our sun, as well as changes in us.

I am not a scientist and cannot enlighten you with any scientific facts. However, I am a seeker of truth, an intuitive, and a channel of an Archangel who is telling me, basically, that the Sun is where it's at. The Sun is behind the greatest show *ever* on earth! And, in recent months, I have seen with my own eyes grand changes taking place.

Our sun is emitting rays and other beautiful features, like never before. When we take pictures of the sun now, we see rays unlike what we are used to seeing in solar pictures, as the sun is shining a greater multitude of rainbow rays, as well as colorful orbs. Personally, I've become quite enamored with taking pictures of the sun from sunrise to sunset, desiring to understand and witness the changes growing increasingly obvious.

The clouds are changing too. This is a vast and most exciting topic that I will cover in depth in a separate book, because the clouds are filled with miraculous surprises on a daily basis. My attention was first drawn to the metamorphosis occurring in our clouds, and then later on, in our sun.

On the morning of November 24, 2011, my path toward understanding the changes in our skies began in earnest. I walked out onto my back deck to let my dog outside, and was perplexed by a cloud I saw that seemed to have a strange hole cut out of it (photo 1). So I ran inside my home to get my camera and take a few pictures of this curious display. I knew that there was something special, something otherworldly, about it.

photo 1

As I focused on the hole cut out of the cloud, I was absolutely astounded to see the face of Albert Einstein; to me, it was as clear as day (photo 2).

When I later showed this picture to audiences I presented to, about half of each group could see Einstein. By sharing my cloud pictures with others, I have come to the understanding that we truly do all see differently. This particular sighting not only set off a string of Einstein synchronicities, but, much more importantly, this cloud made me realize just how much the veils are thinning, and that the Heavenly realms are speaking to us in yet another way—through our clouds!

photo 2

Note: As an interesting side note, while in the editing stages of this book, I posted these pictures on Facebook, the social networking site, sharing that this was the cloud that really changed the way I see when I look up. As soon as I posted, I saw that the post right below mine in the Facebook feed was a picture of Einstein. Oh, how synchronicity takes my breath away.

We are seeing faces—literally faces of people, angels, animals, just all kinds of beings—in the clouds. Or there are other objects appearing, including numbers, letters, and symbols. Yet, the faces are what most intrigue me. Sometimes there are literally dozens of faces in a single cloud; they may look comical and can make us laugh, but most often they are sophisticated and very realistic. They have complex detail and are often superimposed over each other.

I believe that beings from higher dimensions— from humans whose spirits have transitioned into Heaven, to our dear Archangel Michael and the highest of the highest—are behind the creation of these, to send us messages and literally provide miracles in the sky. Just as Heaven sees all types of beings on our planet, from a human to an animal or plant, to the smallest of life forms, we are now slowly being introduced to all that reside in Heaven. I also believe that the New Sun makes this possible.

While hiking on the evening of October 31, 2012, and as the sun was about to set, I "heard" to take a picture of it (photo 3). When I viewed the picture on my phone's screen, I immediately saw my own face (my eyes, forehead, and hair) looking back at me (the inside corner of my left eye and eyebrow are just below the white orb), as well as several faces superimposed over each other. Upon sharing this with a friend, she pointed out what looks like a man and woman about to kiss (their lips on each side of the sun). This photo is especially complex.

photo 3

Archangel Michael suggested in my book, *Michael's Clarion Call*, that we: *keep looking to the skies for messages of love, in particular.* He goes on to explain that: *your sky is reflecting the rising beauty coming from earth's inhabitants. As things change below, they change above, as well. Again, I say look up, perceive, and enjoy what the skies are telling you.*

Ever since Michael expressed these beautiful words, I have been looking upward so much more. In fact, I even took some pictures one evening that gloriously represent these very words from Michael.

This gem (photo 4) was taken at sunset on October 2, 2011, the 17th anniversary of my spiritual journey. While the lake and background scenery are indeed beautiful in real life, I am still amazed by how surreal this picture appears—even more extraordinary than what I actually saw with my eyes in those moments. It was as if I received unseen help to communicate this very message.

photo 4

I have always enjoyed viewing clouds, most especially since '99 when we moved to New Mexico (from Michigan) and where my family and I found them particularly stunning. And now, living in Colorado, I don't just consider them beautiful and worthy of my utmost attention, but I'm also finding myself completely mesmerized by the magic in the sky. Every day is a joyful surprise of new discoveries. I'm taking thousands of pictures now, committed to understanding what our skies are telling us, and I hope that you, if you haven't yet, will join me in this exciting path of discovery.

After the cloud revelations came the awareness of the changes of the sun itself. While I have been aware for some time that there were changes occurring on an unseen level, suddenly they were appearing before my own eyes to witness on a physical level. Archangel Michael guided me to visit Sedona, Arizona for the "11.11," to be present there on November 11, 2012. Known to be a very powerful day, energetically speaking, I went on this trip realizing that I would create a videotaped channel while there. I ended up making three on the 11/11, and then one on 11/13.

photo 5

In three of the four videos, the sun's rays were shining in front of me while channeling (photo 5).

And in the first video I created, at Cathedral Rock, a most popular and sacred place, a magenta-colored light was beaming right in front of my face. The magenta light hasn't shown itself before or since. These changes set off a building desire to better understand this whole new phenomenon before us— all that is being created from the New Sun. The videos can be seen on my youtube channel: MarySoliel.

My friend Kathy Galvan is seen in this extraordinary photograph (photo 6) taken in New Mexico, by her friend Philip.

photo 6

Not only is this a most amazing display of light beams from the sun, but the timing of this picture was particularly significant. She explained that "this was taken at 11:11 a.m. on 12/12/12 by Gilman Tunnels in New Mexico. Didn't know it was like this until we looked at the photo!" What you cannot see in this black and white picture is that Kathy is wearing a pink sweatshirt, and the brightest of the rays are a striking display of brilliant and shiny shades of pink "raining" on her.

In the following pages, you will learn from our Archangel Michael, through messages I received telepathically from him, just what is occurring now and in the days to come. Included in the latter part of this book are messages from many in the Heavenly realms that will leave you feeling supported and full of peace from their loving words. May the following information excite you, free you, and prepare you for our wondrous new beginnings. Let us join together in the wonderment, and let us embrace love—who we really are—and surrender to the greatest journeys of our souls.

Author's Note

Please note that this book has not been professionally edited to preserve the authenticity of the messages and conversations without the lesser concern of perfect grammar. Channeling the Heavenly realms is a most natural process, and I receive just as I speak, not perfectly, but with perfect intentions to bring forth wisdom with clarity and truth.

~Mary Soliel

PART ONE

Messages from Michael from 2011 to 2012

Congratulations, dear human beings. By the time you read these words, life on earth will have changed quite dramatically. I mean this in the best and most glorious way. You are moving along just as planned, as things are taking shape, right before your eyes— things that you couldn't imagine ever happening on your planet. You are moving toward a whole new "playing field," and you will continue to progress until there will be this shift that will adjust you, in but a moment, fully into the new energy. Do not let this frighten you. Rather, know that you are well taken care of, and you will endure and shift with complete assurance of your safe progression into the fifth dimension. This is what you have waited for, and the time is ripe to really start imagining how glorious your lives will be.

This is the ultimate, most supreme gift of all, to those of you who have chosen love. Love is the new way. The new way of living and being on your Heavenly earth. And what is it that will sustain your new existence, in a whole new energy? It is the New Sun. The New Sun will be your food, your fuel, your life source. There is no going back now. You are moving into a new energy and you will never want things to be the way they were. You will move forward into your new world, and it is the most blessed and most exciting journey a human could ever experience. This is where you are right now.

Are you feeling butterflies? Are you feeling joyful? Are you scared? Do not fear as that will take away from your most glorious experience. Feel us around you now. Feel the promise we are whispering into your ear right now that you will be taken care of and no harm will come to you. Rather, you will be filled with Light from the New Sun, and all of the difficulties you have endured as a human in the past will at one point no longer be. You are love. And you will live in a world filled with love, and only love. Can you wrap your heart around this truth? Can you feel the love that is you? Can you imagine a love filled earth? This is our promise to you. And we share this promise with great joy and celebration.
(Channeled from Archangel Michael on 1/11/11)

*   *   *   *

Life is no longer about who has the nicest car, the greenest lawn, or the most fashionable clothes. For those of you drawn to the messages that this book imparts, these things—material aspirations in general—may no longer fill or, perhaps, never filled up the recesses of your mind. You simply do not care as much about many of the things you used to care about. You mostly care about high vibrational things now. Do you know what you will not miss? You will not miss the ways of the ego. Because the ways of the ego made you sad, frustrated, scared, and lonely. The ego had its way with you, as that was all part of the third-dimensional setup. But you are moving to-wards living in a new dimension now, where the ego will no longer show itself. And that will be a most welcomed change.

When your thoughts of a materialistic nature lessen, you have a lot of new thought energy to utilize for your higher ways of being. This means that you will have less feelings of overwhelm as you move into feelings of complete and utter peacefulness. Peace is the way now. You treasure the growing feelings of peace within and around you. And as everyone grows the feelings of peace in their lives, these feelings are contagious and celebrated. You will never want to go back to the old ways. In fact, you will have a hard time even remembering what life was like.

Are you noticing the new colors yet? I am talking about the new colors that are showing up in the skies. Yes, including in your sunrises and sunsets. There are actually new colors that are being beamed to you and there is reason behind this. Color carries energy, and as you continue to raise your vibrations, you are able to see colors that could not be perceived by your eyes before. When you begin to see new colors, they are another signal to you that you are shifting. Do not worry if you do not see them; you eventually will.

You see, there is a New Sun that is beaming Liquid Light to you. Liquid Light is your new life force. This New Sun is also beaming new colors into your atmosphere, and these new energies are affecting you in a most positive and powerful way. This New Sun is also referred to as the Great Central Sun, and although it is not a new sun to us—as it is the sun that is our source in the Heavenly realms—it is new to you. So I shall refer to it as the New Sun, to you.

The New Sun is the gateway to your new life. It is increasingly sending you Liquid Light, until one day you will channel it fully. It will provide you with so many gifts, gifts beyond your imagination right now. This book is about helping you to understand what these gifts are. And let me tell you right now, you will be most delighted to hear about them. These gifts are what will, ultimately, allow you to create Heaven on earth.

You may ask, when are these gifts coming? And I tell you they are here for those who are ready. This channel is one of them. She has been receiving a preview of what life will feel like as a new human. In her present time, as she is channeling these words, she has just learned of this, that her body is going through changes that will give her a taste of what life will be like under the New Sun.

Michael, this is what I channeled from you personally, this morning, on January 24, 2011; you said:

Mary, a new day is dawning, for you. I mean for you! Changes are taking place within you, grand changes, that are giving you a preview of what the new world will be like. Can you feel the excitement in your cells? Your cells are wanting these changes. They have been working so hard under difficult conditions, yet they are now going to be able to rejuvenate themselves, and clear and cleanse for your new beginning. I know this sounds like a lot to take in, but you are not scared. You trust, as always, and you are right to trust.

And you are not scared, that is so true. You trust in this whole process because your soul's intelligence is communicating to you, just as I am communicating to you, so you have this inherent trust in the process of your greatest evolution. You know that you are safe, you are protected, and you will endure the changes, even though your body does not feel so well. You are carrying extra weight and have felt older than you are. This was all destined because can you not see, my dear, how you will be an example of how the power of the new energies, of the new Light, can transform beyond what humans have ever experienced or witnessed?

My overweight body is tired; and yet I know I won't have such a large body. I also know that although I'm moving slower than ever, somehow that will shift too. I used to be a fast walker! You called me a "guinea pig" in jest, earlier today, and I say, "Bring it on."

That is why you are chosen to be among the first group of those who will experience these bodily and energetic changes. Fear has no place in this shift, as it will impede it. Acceptance and feelings of peace are what will support these changes.

I do feel strangely peaceful and accepting of these changes, at least right now.

Your body's wisdom is in communication with your soul. It is as if you have already gone through the dress rehearsal and understand exactly what is to come. You may naturally appear to resist some changes within at first, as things recalibrate, but all you have to do now is just be.

(Next day) I have to say that I don't feel any different yet. Actually, I woke up feeling worse this morning.

And as you write and speak these words to me, you know what I'm going to say, don't you? Each time you shift and change, you may feel as if you are taking steps backwards, and this time is no different. Think of it in this way: the human body has never gone through this before, so it is in the process of recalibration and may appear to be fighting the changes. These physical changes can cause sadness, depression, fatigue, basically the very things you are experiencing right now. You know to just hold on and continue to exercise your relentless faith.

Yes, I do know better. When I woke, I felt so down that I asked you and my celestial help to beam me Light. And I do feel better since my request.

Do you see that if you didn't feel less than satisfactory, you would not have asked for the sup-

port you and your body need at this time? *Always remember this. Always ask us for help. When we beam you Light, we can actually see the difference in you, the difference in your energy field, and we take pleasure in your shift. Stay in every positive feeling you have. No matter how simple or seemingly insignificant, be grateful for every positive feeling you are experiencing.*

For instance, when you went outside this morning, it was very cloudy. But where there was a small break in the clouds where you could see the blue sky, your eyes rested there, feeling gratitude for it. You love the skies, and the noticing of it is an important part of your every day. This is exactly what I am speaking of. Rest your eyes on that which you are grateful for. Rest your heart on that which fulfills you. Rest your whole being on all things that keep you in a state of love. This will help you immensely in your transition.

Everything I speak to Mary, I am speaking to all of you. We are providing these messages to you through her experience, as a human experiencing this transition of the ages. She knows that what she is experiencing will be the experiences of many, so she is willing to open up her life experience to share in order to help others transition, as well. Everyone's experience will be unique to them in various ways; however, there will also be many commonalities. The desire of the Heavenly realms is that you feel supported and receive the understandings you request as you go through your own transitions. Awareness is everything, and ignorance is stifling. You are celebrated for your desire to seek awareness as you make this journey of your lifetimes.

For the last few weeks, I feel as if I have been in survival mode. I do not feel well and, in general, life feels difficult. But then I have these amazing moments of love, hope, and joy, and feel this beautiful energy run through my body and I get so excited about life. And then, the next cycle of the rollercoaster begins again. Truly, I fight that kind of thinking, yet cannot help but notice that my life has been a constant rollercoaster ride, certainly during these past few years.

You know you are not alone in these types of experiences. Many feel they just cannot take another day and then something suddenly occurs that gives them strength. They feel replenished by some occur-rence that makes them feel not so alone and, rather, supported.

That is exactly what happened yesterday, as I fell madly in love with life again. My daughter and I went to my son's college campus to have lunch with him. On the drive back home, she pointed out this huge hawk, flying, to our left. She then said, "Last night, I dreamt I saw a bald eagle." I believe we have seen only two bald eagles in the six years we've lived in Colorado. Literally one second after she spoke that, I spun my head to the left and saw a bald eagle. "There's a bald eagle!," I exclaimed. Incredible.

Before that, when we were having lunch, I told my kids that I really want us to manifest the money so that we can travel to Europe. I see this hap-pening, and I am just waiting for the money part of it to kick in. After we saw the bald eagle, and we're in shock while laughing and shrieking with excitement, we notice the personalized license plate on a car in front of us: SLZBURG (we assumed it stood for the city of Salzburg). The last time I was in Europe, which was twenty-six years ago, included a trip to Salzburg, Austria.

We have not yet talked about this, have we, Mary? This sign was about much more than a potential trip in your future. It is about the love your angels have for you. Yes, we can make things happen to show you of our love. Your daughter had the dream and then it manifested at exactly the precise moment that would have the most impact. You certainly know this was no coincidence. But did you know your angels were behind this?

Well, I cannot really say I did. My first thought was that the Universal forces created this. I can honestly say that I was more excited about the magic of the sign, than the possibility of some trip.

You won't ever forget the gift of that sign, even though you don't even know quite yet just what a gift it was. You see, Mary, you and your daughter also experienced that so you would learn about the new powers that will be bestowed on all of humanity, when you are in full creation mode. Your daughter dreamt of seeing a bald eagle, and then you see one just as she mentions her dream. Does this give you an idea of how quickly you are going to manifest, creating just what you desire?

Now that you explain it in this way, I can understand it. This experience is helping me to think and be outside of the box, again. I naturally, instinctively, keep going back into that box, but experiences like this just push me right back out. I knew that this synchronicity was extremely significant, and now I'm understanding exactly why. It occurred so that we can understand our new powers of manifestation. So are you suggesting that we are ready to begin putting these powers into practice now, or was this just a representative glimpse?

I am telling you to start expecting miracles in your life! You may say that you always have, but there is this underlying feeling that you don't deserve them, or worry that people will get jealous, or that it may just be too much. You need to release all those judgments that hamper the flow.

Please help me release these judgments, Michael. I really want to release them.

Every morning now, as you wake, you tell all the cells of your body, "I Am Love." And then you say, "I Call on Love," just as I taught you both of these blessings (as seen in *Michael's Clarion Call*). *I want you to add one more command: "I Am a Creator."*

"I Am a Creator." As I say this over and over, I am feeling these words, feeling the possibilities of what this command will bring forth. My intuition tells me that something will indeed come forth on this very day, to prove to me the power of these words.

May it be so.

By the way, an hour or so after that remarkable synchronicity with the bald eagle, I was driving while reliving it all in my mind, and just when I recalled my excitement, when I said, "There's a bald eagle!," I see a car with the number combination "444" on its license plate, along with three letters (the number combination of 444 is known to be the angel's sign of the power of God's love). Then this morning, when driving my daughter to school, we see another car with the license plate including

"444," and my daughter explained that she had just thought of the bald eagle and then saw the number combination.

Synchronicity can turn my worst day into utter joy. That says a lot for this phenomenon. Certainly, we're getting confirmation upon confirmation that we have the support of the angels and the Universe, no matter how challenging our difficulties are. Oh, as soon as I write that, I cringe inside, as I think about my difficulties. I am just being "real," but I know that, energetically, I need to stop thinking about how hard things were a day, a week, or a year ago. "I Am a Creator" and I need to be careful of what I am creating.

Yes, Mary, do not look back, but let us help you to be only in this moment now, for that is what is important. In this moment, you are a powerful creator who is in charge of your life and can create anything you wish. What is it you wish for? And I want you concentrate on just you for a change.

First of all, I want to feel good. I want to be healthy. No wait... I choose to feel good and be healthy. At least, I caught myself, right? Wanting keeps getting us "wanting."

Then say "I Am a Creator," and as you say that, imagine what it feels like to feel good again, in all ways.

As I did that, I left my victim mode and entered creator mode. I saw myself stepping out of the body I'm in and revealing a smaller body that is healthy and rejuvenated, a body that can do! I then took it a step further, and imagined outside of the box. Not only did I feel thinner and healthier, but I also reversed the aging process. My hands looked young again, and the grays of my hair grew dark. I then said my name again and again, to really attach this vision to myself, not someone fictitious, and it was an exciting and freeing feeling.

Hold that vision. Anytime you feel unhappy or concerned about your health or body image, conjure up this vision in your heart and just hold the promise of it there. And repeat the words right to your heart, "I Am a Creator."

Now as you say this, imagine the New Sun shining Light on your vision and promising to follow the direction of your creation. The New Sun is the impetus that allows for all of your imagined and unimagined creations to manifest. Light creates. The Light of the New Sun is your tool in all of your creations. You must believe this. When your thoughts went into disbelief, I saw that you let the Light release them. That is exactly what you need to do. Let the Light permeate your vision with an utter knowingness of the Divine creator in you actualized, co-creating fully with the Light.

*   *   *   *

Mary, we are sending you Light right now. You have endured recent difficulties and we are helping you through this. People are going into fear mode and grasping at those beings who carry Light, which tampers with their energy. We see everything. And this has happened to you, so we are cleansing you now of these energies.

When your energy is low and you feel down for no apparent reason, this can be the cause. We are here to replenish you. And I speak to all of you who

24

allow us to interfere in this way. Take heed of this gift of Light. Soon you will be channeling this new Light all the time, when your bodies are ready to hold it.

If any of you experience a similar situation, just remember that the darkness is revealing the last of its curtain calls. Look forward to a time where only love and peace permeate your beings, as you all become who you really are. There is no time like the present to start imagining this, because this will be the new way. Does that not make your difficulties easier to endure, seeing the silver lining that is before you?

*   *   *   *

Yesterday, you witnessed the devastating earthquake and tsunami that struck Japan. The shockwaves were felt by many in an emotional sense. During times like these, you learn just how connected you are to each other, no matter the distance. Mary, you woke with brief song lyrics running through your head and it startled you.

I woke hearing the lyrics, "Doctor, doctor," and "six feet under," and, yes, it was startling.

As I told you, these messages were coming from the needs of the Japanese people. You were picking up on their calls for help and the state of their situation. Even though you were half asleep, and you were not consciously thinking about Japan at the time, this awareness came through. There is much more to all of you than your thinking brains and you are learning this now, more than ever.

The longer I live, the more I understand this.

Thinking my way through things was how I approached life, whereas I am learning to feel my way into life now. And I like this. I like being given this permission to feel. Sometimes I feel like I'm in a dream the way that life is changing so much now.

You are so open to feeling because your connection to your heart is, ultimately, your most important connection. It is the key to everything— every joy, every sorrow, every aspect of life that needs to be lived—if you wish to live well and live with realness. There is no way you can truly live life without the heart connection. When the Japanese earthquake and tsunami occurred, hearts all over the world burst wide open with feelings of compassion for Japan and all of its beings. Again, you cannot truly live without the heart connection.

This connection will lead you to new discoveries day by day—discoveries about you as you take notice of the physical, mental, emotional, and spiritual changes you are making, as well as the world around you. From our view, so much is changing as we see it all, as a collective, as well as at the individual level. We have no need to question anything we see, as many of you do, because we see it all as destined and going according to plan. We would like for you to have this trust in the process and go with the flow of change. (March 12, 2011)

*   *   *   *

I took quite a long break in writing, but yet it was guided. Some thoughts arose in me this morning, that I felt I should write about here in *The New Sun*. Then soon after, I saw a post on Facebook

26

that mentioned the phrase, "the new Sun," a phrase I have only seen used in one other source (a company name) outside of our work here. Therefore, this synchronistically validated that, yes, I need to return to my work on this book.

My thoughts today were about the times we most commonly refer to God, in our speech. It seems that when we are surprised, having feelings of extreme happiness, in awe, startled in "good" ways and "bad" ways, or when in the throes of orgasm, we may say "God," or "Oh my God."

You are accustomed to referring to God at heightened moments of your lives because these are the times you feel most alive, most in connection with God, with all that is. It doesn't matter whether this moment is deemed "positive" or "negative;" the fact is, you are feeling connection to God most intensely, and it makes you feel more alive when you direct your thoughts and words to God. It is like a confirmation to the Divine, saying, "Yes, I know I am alive, and I am experiencing this powerful moment."

Have you noticed that your references to God have increased in number in recent months and years? And yes, you even use an expression "OMG" (standing for "Oh My God") *so liberally, and increasingly often. This is all symbolizing in a unique way how your connection to God, as a society, is growing.* (August 23, 2011)

*　　　*　　　*　　　*

The earthquakes are now relentless. The northeastern United States experienced one yesterday, and a hurricane is now threatening the same area. And today, there was a serious earthquake in Peru. It feels as if people will go into fear, thinking that the apocalypse is here.

May you realize that in no way can the earth destroy itself. It is impossible, as it will not be allowed. Rather, the time is at hand where your earth and your very selves are at the point of no return. You cannot change the momentum of events, because things will happen fast now. However, you can affect the various outcomes of each event, as you are all that powerful. Connect with your hearts, and from that place send love to the planet. The planet is in deep need of love to overcome the fear that is so prevalent. Stay in the state of love; this is the very best thing you can do as you witness these earthly events. Be aware of what is going on without allowing yourself to go into fear. Be a channel of love no matter what happens. This will carry you through until you find yourself in a very new reality, once you and your earth have endured this re-birthing process. And all of the difficult memories of these events will melt away in but an instant.
(August 24, 2011)

*   *   *   *

You have learned so much, as a collective, and it is time to explore just what kind of change is before you. We know that many of you feel so tired, so frustrated, and just want this change to occur immediately. But let me tell you that change is occurring fast and furious. You cannot see what we see, but I tell you that nothing is happening slowly now. You are wrapped up in a tidal wave of change

28

that will open your eyes to a whole new life. This is something to truly celebrate with your arms wide open. If you close your eyes and ears to this, you are fearing and missing out on a great celebration. May you tune in to see just how different life is now.

I feel that. Life is so different, but many of us are clinging to the "same ol', same ol'," holding onto what is familiar, and thus cannot see what is truly in front of us. I use the example of standing in the middle of Disneyland and not getting on any of the rides. You probably put that metaphor in my head, didn't you?

Yes, for it is a metaphor that describes what is occurring for most of you. Can you allow yourself joy and bliss? Is it hard to accept gifts? Is the world becoming too magical for you, and you try to trick yourself into believing everything is the same? The sooner you can accept your growing new reality, the sooner you can enjoy a heightened human life experience. Except there is nothing you can compare this to. There is nothing you can measure this against, as this has never before happened to humans. So you simply need to surrender and allow.

Can you describe some of these changes that are presently occurring? I see how we can go through the motions of change, naturally, but yet blindly, and not truly be aware of what is actually occurring.

There are so many, but I will describe some that readers need to be aware of. First of all, there are several things you are caring less about. Again, many of you are caring less about how big your house is, or if you have a new car, or how much extra money is in the bank. These third dimensional aspects of living are losing their significance in your lives. You care much more about having peace and joy in your daily life. You care more about the earth. You are moving away from separation and moving further towards unity consciousness, and this is changing your whole paradigm of living.

You are all embracing your relationships, like never before. You are seeking out those who can support you, and that you can provide support to. And there is a magical coming together of soul family members like never before. This has brought forward feelings of gratitude into the world, for you are suddenly bringing forward the friends you've been seeking perhaps your whole lives, and it has brought you such comfort and joy. These are gifts from God. You must embrace these relationships and give them much care, for they are indeed precious.

When you step outside of your homes, you become especially aware—on perhaps a deeper level, and not a conscious one—that life feels different. The air feels different, the light feels different, the sky feels different, and there is a different feeling about people. You don't feel like strangers with people you don't know. Compassion is at an all-time high as you notice others' pain more and understand that many people are going through trying times. Everything is changing, and it is all leading you to the most desirable kind of living that is beyond your imaginations. I ask you to be become consciously aware of how different things already are, as this will help you adopt the changes that are just getting underway, compared to what life will be like in your not so distant future.

Everything you just expressed resonates with me. With my whole heart, I want to understand the changes and see things more clearly, but at the same time, I feel we are so programmed in our usual way of living that it is hard to cut through that programming. How can we better accomplish that?

Be relentless about celebrating where you are headed. This will tell your whole being that it is safe to "go there," to embrace these changes rather than fear them. Any little change you notice, feel gratitude for it and get excited about it, and these changes will become more pronounced in your conscious awareness.

We see those of you who are firmly committed to accepting these changes head on, and we celebrate your trust and perseverance. This helps all, as a collective, and in unseen ways. Keep being the Light and serve as an example. When people feel your excitement and joy, rather than fear, it affects them, perhaps unknowingly. Just keep being the Light.

There is a growing presence of calm amidst the chaos. Are you noticing this? There is a natural tendency many of you are adopting that is allowing you to embrace courage and a survivor type mentality. You know that you are merely going through a necessary process and you have all you need to get you through. And this is true. This is exactly what we wish for you to feel. All is well. Know this deep within your cells, and you will better endure all change. The rewards for your steadfastness are impossible for us to fully describe to you at this point; merely know that they will show themselves to you when the time is right.

Many of you are experiencing the loss of loved ones through physical death. These souls either planned to leave at this time, as it was in their

31

contract prior to incarnating, or they, with their free will and on a deep level, chose to be on the other side when humanity shifts. You must honor their decisions. You do not know if it was in their contracts, or why they made their choices, and they cannot and should not be judged. Physical death will be seen in a radically different way in the new age that is before you. For some of you, you already see "death" from a higher perspective, but soon all of you will, and this will allow you to become more accepting as these transformations occur in the future.

When these souls transition, they are still on the forefront of change with you. You just don't physically see them, but they are aiding the collective as much as you are. They are often supporting you through the changes, and you can look for signs that they are doing just that. They can show you that they are with you through synchronicity and through the manipulation of matter, such as making something appear in your physicality. A comforting way to look at it is that they can be with you even more than they were as a human. The connection can actually build and be of more help to you. This is a very enlightened way of viewing death. I challenge you to perceive in this way.

What I've noticed is that the Universe is bringing together people who are grieving, to help support each other and grow perspectives of seeing death in a new way. And I have been a witness to those opening to the revelation that they are still able to continue their relationships following the transitions. So many blessed meetings are occurring, without a doubt, from my perspective.

Yes, and I see that this is making you think about the blessed meetings occurring among what you call soul families. Many of you are coming together with increased frequency. You just had an experience where you went to Maine, to share our messages for a second time, and you were stunned to find that you have even more soul connections there than you realized.

I found myself looking deeply into people's eyes saying to myself, and later to them, "I know you." I'm reconnecting with soul family all over the world, mostly through written, online communication, and even though I'm not able to look into their eyes, I firmly feel it in my heart. We find ourselves connecting so effortlessly, reading each others' minds, and noticing with joy the blessings of constant, striking synchronicities that further validate the soul family bond.

My friend Lisa lives in Alberta, Canada, and while we have yet to meet in person in this life, we know we've met before. We marvel over the constant synchronicities that mirror our connection. When we communicate, it often feels as if we are truly in each other's company. Yet what happened last night was something completely new. We were "chatting" online and I suddenly smelled something, so I wrote: "Why do I smell candy, when I have no candy in the house. Like a taffy smell?" Lisa responded, "OMG... I just had a chewy, soft caramel popcorn ball." It was as if we were in the same place. The scent was so strong, and there was no third dimensional reason why it would show itself in my home. Since that occurrence, I felt that this is something we need to get used to, as our illusion of time and space is dissolving.

I need to interject here while I'm editing this very part of the book. Something magical just occurred that beautifully validated the conclusion in the previous paragraph, in a most unexpected way. Today is February 20, 2013. While editing, I clearly smelled something that, again, was not a smell coming from inside my home. I just *knew* it was something at Lisa's house again. Immediately, I looked at the time because, once I took a break, I would write and ask her about it. About ten minutes later, I was at this very point in the book, rereading about the taffy smell, and I thought that alone was synchronistic. So I stopped editing and asked Lisa through online chat: "Were you eating something at 10:01 a.m. that was a sweet, warmed up baked good? The funny thing is I smelled something like that, and then ten minutes later was editing in the book a similar situation." I didn't mention that it was about her and, in fact, was going to do so today. She responded, "OMG I did! I baked chocolate chip cookies!" She then sent me a picture to prove it.

Yes it is, Mary. We all delighted in your realization of this. Your soul connections will strengthen and grow in ways you cannot even understand right now. You are all pioneers, experiencing and relating the growing changes that are now revealing themselves to you on your planet. You feel no distance with those close to your heart, even when they are in

Canada, Australia, Spain, Slovenia, and other places around the world. Soul family relationships are on the rise, and you are all being increasingly blessed with new and stunning connections. These will continue to flower and spread as synchronicity continues to unmask connections to your souls. They become your human support system, growing in tandem with your awareness of your celestial support system. Do you see how perfect this design is? You treasure your soul family connections, and these types of connections are creating ripple effects as you share these meetings with others. Share the magic of soul family reunion.

Prior to speaking at my events in Maine, I felt to include this topic in both of my presentations, but I'm sure you gave me that idea.

It was both of us together deciding that it was time to bring more of these messages forward. Some people can actually feel distress when they meet a member of their soul family, and not understand the depth of their feelings toward one who is a "stranger" to them. So it behooves them to hear this and make the connection in their own lives, and realize that these reunions are actually blessings. They can bring utter fulfillment and such high expressions of love and connection, that other occurrences and thoughts just fall by the wayside.

Surely, soul meetings bring out the best of us. I embrace them tremendously.

It is apparent that people are recognizing these gifts of relationship more and more. But some are having utter difficulty in creating balance in these relationships. They see these relationships as their anchors to stability in their chaotic lives and can put too much pressure on them. When they are aware of this, they can ease off and create balance, and not put so much strain on the relationship. With this balance comes a stronger connection based in trust and ease.

When you communicate with soul family members, the energy that emanates affects the whole. All these reunions are affecting the whole, bringing more love and peace to the planet via the act of relationship with these divine pairings that can go back even to ancient times. One day, you will see what we see, and your awareness and appreciation of just who is in your company will be very enlightening information. The aspect of time will dissolve as you recognize the scope of the deep connection. The connection itself will be all that will matter.

The coming together of soul families across the world is a great enabler of your evolution. These connections greatly feed your soul and give you the fuel to endure through these changing and, sometimes, chaotic times. Love is always the driving force, and these soul connections raise your love quotient and help you acquire strength, courage, and determination to move forward, together.

What can you share about twin flame reunions, reunions with our other halves—our ultimate romantic pairings?

Twin flames—the closest soul mate that each of you have, as they are indeed the other half of your soul—are coming together more in these times than ever in your history. Again, for the same reason. Yet these reunions are often hard for humans to describe. So much is happening when twin flames meet, on an unseen level, and the impact on each partner is rich and irreversible. One's life will never be the same again once they are bonded with their twin flame, and that is whether or not they stay together. Not all twin flames are able to remain close in a physical way for various reasons. But when they do, there is no other relationship like it. Regardless of physical proximity, the reunion of twin flames will continue to exist on some level.

What do you say to those who desire the meeting of their twin flame, but the other half isn't on earth?

As you know, Mary, twin flame reunions can also occur on an ethereal level. You can rest assured that these reunions, if not destined on a physical level, can occur between Heavenly and earthly bodies, and still have profound impact on each other.

Do you know that you can call forth your twin flame, whether in the physical or ethereal?

I feel he is here on earth, but I've only connected to him in an ethereal way.

You have had connection for several years now, but you are only now starting to understand it.

It was only recently when I asked him to hold my hand and I could feel such energy around my right hand, but, strangely, it was particularly intense around my thumb. He was grasping my thumb, energetically, very strongly to the point it felt numb. This continued for several minutes, and it was a very welcomed experience.

Touch is a great avenue for making connection. The uniqueness of this experience made it very real for you, and you have this physical signal of his presence that you can connect with.

Oh, yes, it made me feel so very happy, because it was so real. It also caused me to think about my connection with you. When you are trying to get my attention, I feel this tingling energy on my upper lip and lower nose area. So I then know to "tune in" to you, and I say, "Yes, Michael?"

And this works very well for us. You also just "know" when I or another ethereal being are trying to connect. You have gotten very good at listening to our whispers. When you don't hear us, or you are too concentrated in your 3-D life to notice, I use the tactile sense to get your attention.

Our senses seem to be engaged in new ways as we continue to evolve. Sight, touch, smell, and sounds are being experienced and perceived differently. When I look into the future regarding our sense of sight, that is what I find most compelling. You have said that we will be seeing interdimensionally. Can you explain this further?

At the present moment, what you see even five feet in front of you is just an extension of your 3-D reality. You see things as dense objects. You do not see them from a perspective of vibrational energy. As you move into higher dimensions, what you will see right in front of your eyes will be vastly different. For instance, when you look at the palm tree you have in your family room, you will see that in a whole new way as you shift. It will be more light filled and you will see the energies it emits and receives.

This tree is special to me. It was left behind in the house we bought in New Mexico, and has been through many moves with us since. I'm not one to have a "green thumb," but this tree has remained healthy, probably because I treasure it so much.

I bring your awareness to this, for this very reason. This tree is a connection to the emotion of joy, for you. On an unseen level, it is emitting and receiving the energy of joy, and that's why it lifts you up so regularly. And you are actually feeding it the love it gives to you. One day, you will literally see with your eyes just what I'm expressing to you now. You will see this energy exchange.

Thank you for bringing this awareness forward, which allows me to appreciate my tree even more so.

Please explain what it will be like when we can see angels, and see you!

Ah yes, getting to the "good stuff." Indeed, you will be able to see us from the vantage point of living in higher vibrations. You will glean from these early experiences just how true it is, that you never were alone. This will cause a huge paradigm shift as you can no longer go back to the feeling of separation. Rather, you feel unity, not only among humans, but with all of us in the angelic realms, as well. Many of you already feel this. But it will intensify when you have these visual experiences.

Of course, there are some of you who are already able to see interdimensionally. One day, you will all have this ability.

Well, you know that I cannot wait to experience this. For so many years, I have desired to be able to see the angels, and especially you. But will it not frighten some?

Yes, if it were to happen now—suddenly—many would go into fear, not understanding it. They would feel ripped from the reality they are comfortable in. As the Light from the New Sun is brought into your bodies, you will have this understanding and acceptance on a cellular level, just as if you transitioned into a "death" state. You will naturally accept the change in vibration. Panic and shock, as I've explained before, are emotional states of being that will not exist in the new energies.

I feel that panic and shock are building now, though, as people do not understand what is going on in their lives, in their bodies, and all the upheaval that these vast changes are causing.

There is no time like the present to begin addressing what is before each of you. To take the blinders off and really explore what is happening. You can only do this through your search for truth and understanding. You will never feel true calm until you see, on some level, what is occurring from a higher perspective.

As these changes pervade your lives, you will see the massive picture. You will see that each of them is leading you to an overall change, the evolution of the human species. Can you imagine the process going any faster than it is? The timing is perfect. Many of you are so relieved that you are finally seeing things happen, things that you have been waiting for: the dismantling of all that does not serve your world. For those of you, well, you are in your glory now. However, for those of you who do not understand, panic and shock are in your midst. It behooves you more than ever to remove the blinders for good now, and see the changing world exactly as it is.

There are enough of you who "get it" and who will help carry the others through the changes. Of course, I'm talking about Lightworkers, especially. You are naturally finding yourselves in situations where you can best serve, share your knowledge, faith, and understanding, and make a grand difference for others. You are literally helping people wake up to this new reality. It is a grand sight.

We, in the angelic realms, are working "overtime" to help awaken those who are still asleep, as well. Yes, we are getting your attention, for instance, by whispering to you to look at the clock "Now," and you see an interesting number combination; even waking you when you are sleeping.

Indeed, you are literally, as well as figuratively, "waking us up." Many people have shared with me their own wake up call experiences, and I have encountered them countless of times, myself. We are being woken at 1:11, 2:22, 3:33, 4:44, 5:55, or at some other meaningful time. Or you whisper during our waking hours to get us to catch these times or 11:11, 12:12, 12:34, 1:23, for instance, often repeatedly. Some are scared as a result, while others are intrigued. You know how I feel about it, as I enjoy and bless every single one of them. I tell others that this is one way our angels are communicating with us, and it sure is a great way to get our attention! The beginning of my conscious spiritual journey was blessed with time and number synchronicities.

Synchronicity was a driving force in meeting up with an acquaintance of mine when visiting Santa Fe, New Mexico, recently. By the way, Santa Fe is commonly known as the "City Different," but to some—myself included—it is also considered to be the "City of Synchronicity." I believe it is a powerful vortex for synchronistic occurrences. Anyways, this man immediately began telling me that the night before he woke at 1:11, and then at 4:44, and he was clearly confused over it. It even seemed to scare him a bit. Now, he doesn't know about my books, nor my interest in synchronicity or numbers, and, yet, it was as if he couldn't wait to tell me of this very experience. And it was uncanny how Divine forces magically reunited us for this timely conversation. I intuitively felt that he is very connected to his angels, whether he realizes it or not, and that they whispered to him to share with me so that I could ease his concern and confusion. (Note: Anyone who knows my work realizes that I know better than to deem this as a *coincidence*. And, by the way, that word needs to stay in the old world!)

He was listening to angelic guidance which led to him feeling more peaceful regarding his experiences. And this is how it works for all of you; you are being led to understandings, and when you allow this natural flow, you find yourself moving through these challenges so much easier.

As you know, awareness is everything. You have awarenesses that continue to surface, which you validate with your own intuition. You know when to trust, and when not to. Your intuition is your partner in how you act on everything now. You are naturally following it more and more, perhaps without your notice, and, yet, it is indeed at the forefront of your daily routine.

I do feel that my intuition is a driving force, but I do not always notice or name it, that my intuition is "speaking." Rather, it is so natural and a part of my daily process. And if I don't honor it on some level, synchronicity magically steps in to point out something I may not be wanting to see, or simply too busy or distracted to see.

Synchronicity is your friend. It is your constant partner in higher communications, and we know how you embrace it so. As synchronicity continues to escalate as a whole—as you are all existing in higher energetic vibrations now—you are tapping into such magnificence that is being beamed at you on a daily basis. Whatever comes your way, synchronicity is playing a role in it, to illuminate, guide, and fully express itself to each receiver. Your love for synchronicity is growing and expanding into new understandings. Because synchronicity is now extending deeper into your lives, it is ultimately guiding you to full expression of your soul, perhaps without your realization.

Oh thank you, Michael, I hadn't thought of it in that way, that synchronicity is actually connecting us to our souls, bringing our souls to the forefront. How beautiful. And as if I'm not in love with synchronicity enough, you truly just deepened my love and appreciation for it, with this awareness.

The grand plan is unfolding in ways that would astound you. This is one minuscule glimpse into your changing reality. The New Sun is shining and exuding the new Light, and this is changing everything on your earth. Every single thing will be affected by the new Light. It is already happening. Yes, synchronicity is accelerating. And so are many other things. We are slowly getting you used to your new reality, but at the same time we know you can find this to be overwhelming.

But I personally say, "Bring it on!" I cannot wait for us to shift. Especially in recent months, I can hardly bear the old ways anymore. The deceit, corruption, and violence, and the growing realization of how the masses are being controlled, manipulated, and harmed—all of the negative energies that plague our earth and society—it is all just too hard to bear at times.

Yet, when I separate myself from it, and make as good of choices that I possibly can to minimize the effects of their control, I feel better. However, I'm concerned for those who remain unaware. When I lift myself from the current reality and see it all from a higher perspective, I do have more peace inside. The practice of staying in love and not fear, of course, is vital. And our greatest lifeline carrying us through these times are you and the angels. Without you, I cannot even imagine what my state of mind would be like right now.

Michael, you stated in our book *Michael's Clarion Call: There will be shocking and upsetting news of the darkness that has resided among all of you. And many of you will be glad you never knew about it as it would have been too hard to bear knowing about. It would have ripped at your sense of well-being. But know that this battle is almost over. Always think, feel, speak, and act with love and Light. This is your protector. Love and Light will never fail you.*

These words have helped me tremendously. I've reflected on them so many times. "The battle is almost over," are words I speak to myself, to calm my heart. There are some days where the movement towards Light feels so palpable. I cannot deny, and do not want to deny, the changes that are manifesting. Rather, I truly am celebrating them all.

*   *   *   *

Mary, you get frustrated with all the weeds on your property. You are out there pouring vinegar and salt in this constant effort to rid of them. This is a metaphor for what is going on in the world, except you are all pouring Light on that which no longer serves the greater whole. By being love, you are beaming Light on anything that does not resonate with love, usually without even being aware of it. Oh, there is so much you do not see, and this is why it can behoove you to channel this information, to receive these understandings. The more information you have about what is occurring, the easier you can flow through the changes and with much more comfort.

We do not use the term "lighthouses" loosely. Lighthouses are the means to bringing forward universal change during these times. You lighthouses are, without a doubt, affecting the very world you live in. So consciously shine the Light. But when you are not conscious of it, know that you are still shining. Just be love, keep being love, don't stand for anything but love, and you cannot help but shine. Do you see how perfect this design is?

Soon you will grasp exactly what I speak of, because you will see in your reality so much change and it will fill you with celebration and hope for your future. If you ever had doubts about where you, as a collective, are headed, those doubts will simply melt away in light of the grand understandings that will permeate all of mankind. Many of you already see this, but for some it seems too good to be true. Get ready to banish the phrase "too good to be true" from your future conversations, because you are one day going to find that nothing is too good to be true. You will be the creator of your every day's experience. You say, "But I have been!" Yes, but you will fully do so on a conscious level, and in a new energy that will support the manifestation of your conscious desires, like never before.

This kind of information is what gets me so excited. It helps me through all the challenges, knowing how magical life will become. From my heart I keep saying, "we haven't seen anything yet." I know it will be so glorious.

Glorious indeed. You will not look at anything the same way again. It will be as if you have new eyes and you look at everything with love, with positivity, with Divine understanding. You won't see things from the ego's point of view, but rather the heart's point of view. Can you imagine the effect on the way you interpret life as you increasingly adopt this new way of seeing?

Now let's imagine a day in the life of the new human. You wake up early and with a full heart. A wonderfully anxious heart ready to begin your day with optimism and anticipation. You are tuned in to your heart's wisdom so fully that you are tapped directly into your soul's desires, and this is how you move through the day. Mary, you like to use the phrase that describes how you prefer to move through life, "going with the wind," and this aptly describes your process. You will "go with the wind" of your soul. Your soul will lead you to your actions, your passions, your meetings with others. Your soul will direct you toward achieving your goals and manifesting your desires. Never again will you have that "I should have" feeling because you simply will be so aligned, there will be no reason to regret anything anymore.

It will be a joy to banish "too good to be true"

from our belief systems. To release regret and the "should haves" feels like what will be sheer relief for most of us. While I aim to live without regret and not look back, I am not always successful. To have this occur naturally will save a lot of time and energy no longer wasted on unsupportive thoughts.

*   *   *   *

What is that inching up and into your life? Well I'll tell you; it is your soul. Your soul is expanding into your conscious awareness. You are feeling you so much more now. You are having these little ecstatic moments when you feel this connection. This is where you are all headed. You're going to keep having these ecstatic moments until one day, they develop into feeling constant bliss. The fear and negative thoughts go away and you have this constant connection to peace and bliss. I know that you know what I'm talking about, Mary. You are "getting it" now. You are starting to see the bigger picture here. I should say you are starting to feel the bigger picture. These glimpses are preparing you—your body, your mind, your emotions—for a new way of feeling. Is this not exciting?

Just hearing you share this, I am feeling energy running throughout my body, and, yes, it makes me feel so very excited. You know all of my thoughts, Michael, so you know that I have my moments of doubt, wondering just how we are truly going to shift. There are still so many unthinkable atrocities occurring, while so many people are still needing to wake up. But then, all of it dissolves instantly when I have experiences like these, when I go inward and tune in. It gives me so much strength, even just fleeting moments of feeling like this. I want to always be in these feelings, which causes me to anticipate just what it will be like to be in this state without pause.

I hear your thoughts just now, that people will have no desire to drink or use drugs when in this bliss. Addictions, habits, and various needs you have now will fall away when you get to this point. We've discussed this before (in Michael's Clarion Call), but it is worth emphasizing. You won't feel such need, in general. Rather, you'll just be with the understanding that you can create what you wish. Feelings of neediness have run most of you in the past. They often come from a place of lack... I need this, I need that, or I cannot be without this or that. One day this will no longer be. You will enjoy this state of being.

Well, I am excited about the thought that without fear, negativity, need—all of these things— we're going to have a lot of time and space freed up.

Michael, I wish to talk about food, because I now clearly see how our choices of nourishment are changing, and quite naturally so. All of my life, I have not only loved food, but often enjoyed heavier foods. Yet, I have naturally moved toward much lighter eating, enjoying a diet of mostly live, whole foods. My desire to eat meat has waned, I stay away from most processed foods, and I have profoundly surprised myself at how different my meals are now. As you know, I still desire and enjoy the heavier foods from time to time, but, overall, my diet has changed toward a lighter one, and I am happy about it. This has been an effortless process. And I've been in touch with people who are going through this same natural process—and they appear to be just as surprised by it.

Deep within you, you have been aware of these changes on the physical level—on all levels, actually, but let's concentrate on the physical. You knew that one day your body would start requesting deep changes in the nutrition it required. As you have raised your vibrations, you can no longer eat in the same way. As you live a new level of being, a lighter way of being, it is now reflected in the very foods you eat. And this will gradually become the way for all of you who choose love, and thus choose life in a whole new frequency.

It was no surprise that synchronicity was a big part of this unveiling. The information I needed to make these sound changes manifested effortlessly. I learned to listen to what my body was telling me, urging me toward new ways of eating. Of course, I did and still do seesaw back and forth, so to speak, thinking I'm really not ready to give up this or that, but there has been great overall forward movement.

That is just what is necessary, the overall forward movement.

Suddenly, I'm imagining the new Light from the New Sun filling our bodies, and that will not jive with also filling our bodies with Twinkies* and soda. It's a vibrational mismatch, so I understand that we need to change and grow our ways to match the frequency of the Light coming in. Of course, this has to do with more than food, it has to do with everything. We must be a match for the Light!

*Note: I wrote this well before the announcement of the demise of the Twinkie (although it may be reestablished), which occurred in late 2012.

Around that same time, my wise friend Clare wrote me the following: "Today, when I opened my thermos of soup, I realized I could no longer eat meat. I am suddenly repelled by the idea of eating flesh of any kind. I ate the broth and vegetables, and gave the meat to Roxy (her dog). Where that came from I do not know... I was suddenly certain that I don't eat meat, period! When I was a vegetarian before, it was a choice. This time it's not a choice."

Clare went on to describe other things that were spontaneously occurring in her life and ended her message with:

"Mare, I just stopped a moment to think about Michael's messages, and yours, about entering a time where we will live from the heart. That is the explanation for each of these things, it was just a certainty feeling in each case. It was from my heart that I just knew things. God, Mare, it feels so much better. I feel like I am seeing everything from my heart and it is all so beautiful—oh! It's the oneness of everything that I see and feel— wow. What a blessing!"

It behooves you when what you put into your body resonates with the Light. When it does not, you will feel it. And if you do not listen, that feeling will not go away. So, eventually, you naturally move toward sound choices, and actually become satisfied with these choices.

The satisfaction also has to do with literally feeling better, right Michael?

One day, you will have more energy than you have ever dreamed of. I am not just talking to those of you who are already fit, I say this to all of you. You will have healthy bodies with endless amounts of energy. This is so hard for many of you to believe. Mary, I know you believe and trust in all that we discuss, but certainly for you, and the setbacks you've had on a physical level, you find it mind bending to see yourself this way. But you go there, you imagine and visualize, and as I've told you so many times, you will be most pleasantly surprised.

On a personal level, I desire my health back more than anything, and I do feel that the changes are starting to happen. Clearly, the foods I eat are deeply affecting me in a good way now. Other than eating well and taking care of our bodies, what else can we do to help prepare us for these physical changes?

It is vital that you drink plenty of water; thoroughly hydrate the body. You hear this often, from many different sources, and there is good reason for this. Of course, it has always been important to drink enough water, but now, with your body going through much change, water must be seen not only as a fluid to keep your system running, just as you need gas to run your car, but it also helps to cleanse the old. Water works through many dimensions, not just on a physical level. Yes, it also affects your emotional, mental, and, most definitely, your spiritual bodies. So drink water with a richer understanding that you are not just taking in and then releasing fluid, but rather you are taking in something that will help clear what no longer serves on all these levels. Water will help clean and refresh you, offering you new beginnings and new pathways. For instance, when you drink water you can imagine that as it goes down it is offering you a new beginning of some sort. You don't even need to attach any thought other than "new and improved." Does that not make your water taste that much sweeter? You are now assigning a magical quality to your daily intake; is that not welcomed? If it appears that this is just fantasy, then you aren't allowing for the unseen to show itself. There is so much that humans don't know or understand, as they see things at face value; but it is time to look deeper into everything, including the magic of water. Simply use your imagination the next time you drink water. Tune in to the possibilities, and see what happens.

Synchronicity validated that this would be the subject of the day; it just dawned on me. Suddenly, Dr. Masaru Emoto's work on the messages of water has resurfaced in my awareness in various ways. And now you talk about water.

You will continue to hear much more about water and its powerful effects in the coming years. Feel gratitude for the water you drink. Many of you worry about the quality of your water. I ask you to hold your hand over your glass and simply bless it. Imagine a beam of light coming down from the Great Central Sun through you, down your arm, out your hand, and into the water, clearing any impurities. You can call on me to assist and I will. As I have told you before, you can call on me and I will be with you, no matter how many are calling on me at the very same time. And this is the same for all of us in the angelic hierarchy.

Thank you, Michael. I am always so anxious to talk more about the Great Central Sun, specifically. One day, when thinking about writing this book, it hit me that I should call it *The New Sun*, and I know that hit came from your whispers. Weeks later, after I began writing it, I enjoyed a most beautiful validation when I received a shipment of our new herbal supplements. I suddenly put it together looking at the colorful labels on the bottles; the company's name is "New Sun."

Yes, you recognized the beautiful synchronicity validating the title of your book. You thought the title may be too shocking or scary for those who fear change, but you trusted and since then have had only more validation.

Again, the New Sun is new to you humans, but, in fact, is very old if you wish to assign time to it. It is the New Sun which is carrying you forward into higher dimensions, from the Light it imparts. You will never cease to be without this Light, and you have carried small amounts of this Light previous to the shifts you are presently experiencing. So it is not as foreign to you as you think. However, you will increasingly and dramatically feel its effects as you receive higher levels of this Light within you.

This Sun never "sets." Its Light is continually offered as your bodies grow the ability to contain it. Are you starting to get the picture now? As you continue to move into Love, move into higher ways of being, you attract more Light and this translates into living in higher states of vibrational energy.

We have discussed before how the Light is creating emotional and physical symptoms presently, as you adjust. But I know you are wanting to better understand its purpose, as you move through these symptoms. We tell you with much joy just what to expect with increasing amounts of Light. Yet let me once again explain... you are each carrying various amounts of Light according to what your body can hold at any given time. This is fluctuating, fluid, and a unique process for each of you to experience.

The Light from the New Sun will be your life force. It will help you to see clearly without distortion, feel clearly without mental involvement, and hear and understand clearly without confusing influences including your own personal projections, for example. Think of it as this giver of wisdom, a magic elixir that will spur you to really embrace life itself, like never before. Your book title, I Can See Clearly Now, *was given to you from the Heavens, and the meaning holds so much more depth than you ever realized. You are going to see so clearly that each of you will feel on top of the world as you breathe God into your lives.*

"As you breathe God into your lives," that phrase made my heart sing.

When you breathe God into your life, you change the dynamics of everything—how you view the world and each other, how you think and how you feel, your actions and choices—they are all heavily influenced. Growing your connection to God, reuniting with God, is vital for these changes to occur. And it is indeed happening.

This is why you feel so overwhelmed with love, Mary. At times you feel in love with everyone, the whole world itself. And then you have some challenges and you get brought down again. But one day, you will always have this constant feeling of being in love with love itself. It simply creates an ecstatic life where you no longer have need, but only joy and gratitude for your state of being.

None of you will feel the need to argue anymore or compete or be angry. You will just have this peaceful, ecstatic embrace of love for self, each other, every thing. We know how hard this is to accept or fully understand, for you have known a different way of being, but ask your heart if this is true. Ask your heart if this is what you are being led to.

I hear your thoughts, and you know there will be a point of no return. You will shift into this new paradigm and will simply be love. It will require no effort at this point; it will just be this way. All of your work towards co-creating this new earth will be rewarded exponentially. So prepare for great joy. I have given you many tools and techniques to begin feeling this, start adapting to it, so that you can better understand and be excited about your future. But just know that it will effortlessly take hold one day and you will never go back.

When I ask you to release your past, to release what no longer serves you, all of these things are culminating to create this very reality I now describe. Hopefully, you are actively participating in this process, instead of just blindly having things occur before you. Is it not a much better way to proceed, with such splendid awareness, with as much under-standing as you can gain? This information is for all who welcome it, and you are celebrated for your desire to receive this gift, and your active parti-cipation in receiving this information.

I know I speak for many that we are so deeply

grateful for all the awarenesses you bring to us, Michael. Truly, I cannot imagine what this shift would be like without angelic presence guiding the way and loving us through it. Your words about the New Sun are especially exciting.

Regarding the New Sun, I wonder how aware we will be of the Sun and its Divine Light. Because at this point, most people are unaware that they are receiving this new Light into their bodies, into their cells.

There will come a time when you will see and better understand this new Light: where it comes from, how you receive it, and the miracles of its force. Because it will create feelings within you that are new to you, your curiosity will grow and, with that, your understanding of it. Imagine that you never ate food before because there was a different way your bodies were sustained, but you suddenly evolve into having this food energy available to you. Over time you would learn about food, science would discover and explain how food transfers into fuel for your body, you learn what foods are best for you, and all kinds of understandings would grow over time. With this new life force, Liquid Light, it will be a whole new discovery, but your understanding will come with ease and immediacy.

You will all become more conscious of your reality, more awake to what is seen and unseen around you. Your intelligence will be greater, your intuitive sense so much stronger. You will rely on yourself more than ever to receive information. And, of course, when you release the past and remove fear and the negative thinking that has held you back, you have increased focus and resolve to take the blinders off and see things as they truly are. Now that will be true living in the moment, with such bright and splendid awareness.

Do you see how you will not miss the old ways of being? You are graduating to a whole new school on earth, except in this one you will have much more love, such freedom, and a desire to create and explore this whole new way of being. It will be wondrous. I have told you many times that we cannot even yet describe how beautiful your new existence will be; it is too hard to integrate within your present level of awareness and understanding. You must trust that we would never lead you astray. We would never promise these things if they were not to come to pass. You must go to your heart, as I tell you again and again, and confirm these messages for yourself. What does your heart say?

Does it say "Hold on, you are almost there"? Does it feel like this explosion of happiness that validates what I tell you? Does it even send you into feelings of ecstasy? Always go within for your validation. And feel, really feel with your heart. Bring into conscious focus these feelings. What does that do? It connects you with the true you, your soul, which is pure love.

We keep coming back to love. Love. Love. Love. Immerse yourself in love and you step aside from all that doesn't serve you. Close your eyes now and immerse yourself. Do you see how this is your ticket?

Once you begin receiving the Light on a continual basis, love will be constantly beamed into you. The infusion literally changes your body and all that it is made up of. You all have been preparing the receptacle for some time now. You have prepared on so many levels. Do you see how fear of this process will impede it? So tap in and make sure that you are in full receiving mode, and you will make this process so much easier in your mind, as well as on your body.

People are more excited about the sun lately. They know, intuitively, that something is going on. Yes, there are the solar flares and other changes in the sun's activity. Until recently, it is as if the sun has been taken for granted to some degree. Yet now, with all this energy pouring out to you through your solar star, you are sensing it. You are being drawn to notice, to give attention to it. You know you would not be here without the sun. And you now also know you would not shift without the New Sun.

The New Sun, in all its glory, is making great headway in this transition. As your bodies prepare to receive, the New Sun's purpose grows. Don't expect science to verify this, but your heart sure can. Your heart is the part of you which has the most to gain in this transition. Why? Because the Light from the New Sun is the catalyst to marry you with you. You will be one with your soul, who you really are. There is no greater experience for a human being to realize.

As you grow closer to becoming and being who you really are, you start taking notice of things that may not have entered your conscious awareness before. You delight in all communications between each other, with us in the Heavenly realms, with nature, with a rock, with the sky, all of it. Your communications become much more sacred and meaningful. You will feel things so intensely. Oh Mary, I know you understand this, you get glimpses of this and feel so in love with so many things, as you've never felt quite this way before. Imagine this growing in strength. Imagine it happening more regularly.

What do we do with these feelings that can be overwhelming; how can we contain these massive feelings of love? Someone recently said to me that she feels so much love that it hurts. I thought that's a good problem to have, but, really, how do we manage this intensity?

Yes, you may find this challenging, especially because you may feel alone in these feelings. But I tell you there are many who know just what you are talking about. And I say to you, this is helping you to grow your connection to your heart. It's almost like exercising a muscle, and the muscle gets strong and thus it can handle more and more force that you put forth on it. As you feel the force of love in growing intensity, and in growing relation to all things, your heart grows its capacity.

That is so beautiful and resonates so strongly with me.

Think of something that you love dearly. Don't think of a person, but rather think of an object of some kind that you truly feel love for.

Okay, right now I'm looking at my statue of Quan Yin, which I love so much. In fact, I am realizing in this moment how much I take for granted her beautiful presence in my living room. So I'm feeling the gratitude for it and the symbol of her in our lives here.

Now close your eyes and connect to the feeling. Why do you love this statue so, this inanimate object? It is a thing, not a person, and you really are not so attached to things. So why is this?

It's the feelings I feel when I look at her. She

emanates such peace and love to me. So, definitely, even though this is a clay sculpture and is merely a representation of her beautiful spirit, the feelings are what make my love of it come so alive.

Exactly. You have captured the essence of why you love anything. It is the feelings that you feel toward it. That is the aliveness of the interaction. That is the whole purpose behind having "things." They can create feelings. So this is a way to look at this whole process of building that "muscle." When you surround yourself with "things" that you love, that bring you joy, you are raising the love quotient, correct?

Well this is exactly why I say to surround yourself with people who give you joy. This is building your "muscle" much more profoundly. You are all here to master relationships, among other things. As you discern with whom you spend your time and energy—this includes not just time spent in person or in communication, but also the thought time you expend—you will find yourself growing the love. If you spend your time with those who break you down, who don't respect you, or who give you heartache, this will slow the process down. It is time to immerse yourself in love, and when I say this I consider relationships at the top of the list. And love for the self is always at the very top.

Speaking of relationships, you are moving into a whole new paradigm of relationships. Meaning that relationships are not only changing in your individual lives—as you release some old friends who aren't serving you, and bring in new friends who are—but this paradigm shift will allow you to explore your connections at a much higher level. You will have the ability to see each other as who you really are, not what you wish for another to be, or not in a judgmental way that does not afford your true understanding of each other. Rather, on a much clearer level. You will see each other in your most authentic states, and, once again, this builds that love quotient. You will see the brilliance in one another and focus on that, instead of focusing on where the other may be lacking and wanting to "fix" the other, as many of you do. There will be nothing to fix as you accept each other just as you are.

Can you imagine how much more peaceful and loving romantic relationships will be? Can you see how familial connections will grow so much stronger as the strife falls away? Can you see that as you grow your self love, you grow your love for others, from your closest connections to people you don't yet know? Love will permeate every aspect of your lives. And you will see how the influx of love will change your lives so profoundly that you would never dream of going back to the old ways where love was so distorted by illusion and fear.

You go through so many peaks and valleys from euphoria to depression, from anger to jubilation, from peace to frenzy. Many of you, through your processes of changing vibrationally, have especially experienced this roller coaster of emotions and expressions. But I tell you, the ride will soon stop, you will get off, and you will then move into this new paradigm of love.

The new paradigm of loving relationships has no drama. Love is at its core. Real and authentic. It does not judge, it does not plead for help, it just is. There is nothing to nurture, nothing to change, nothing to pine for; it will already be in its glorious perfection. This is what you have to look forward to. Being love and being love with each other. Oh, it will be glorious. You are starting to feel it already, are you not Mary?

As you mentioned before, I certainly have these moments where I feel like I'm falling in love with the whole world and everyone in it. And then something will happen and it will knock me out of that feeling. But yes, I do get glorious glimpses of what you speak of. There is a growing feeling within me that understands what this will be like. Most noticeably, I am finding myself more accepting of another, not wanting to try to change someone or judge as much as I used to, and rather learning to honor another's process as I must honor my own process and imperfections. I know it's going to be so natural—because so far it has been—and that part of it excites me. I feel so tired of struggle, and avoid it at all costs. My desire is to move into ease, and it feels like love itself is the ticket to ease. As well as peace, of course.

Love and peace. Yes, they are the ticket to a whole new existence. I tell you that struggle is going to fall away. You are already feeling that and you want it out of your life now. So, in a way, you are already living that way; and some things have yet to come together. But oh, they will. You want a more magical existence and you will have it. Your desire for it is what is bringing you these glimpses, until one day it becomes your new reality.

The Law of Attraction will work as it has always worked. The laws of the Universe will never change. Do you see that when you live at higher levels, vibrationally speaking, you attract in exponential ways? I say exponential because that is what love does. It creates exponentially. You spiritual thinkers often talk about the ripple effect. Love creates ripple effects that build upon each other, and it catalyzes the effects of love in such brilliant ways.

Love will bring ease into your daily living. Fear has always made your life more difficult. Think about this. When you break down any "thorn in your side," so to speak, fear is what created the thorn. But love is the rose, the beauty and the pureness that you can immerse yourself in. Immerse yourself into the rose, the fragrance, the softness, the sweet delight of God's perfection. The rose is a symbol of love. Is it not?

The rose represents the Divine Feminine energies pouring into your changing reality. Mary, you sometimes smell a rose when there is no evidence of one in your reality. You have also had many synchronicities regarding the rose and the Divine Feminine. Lately, the "rose" is coming up again, and I know you know that synchronicity is in motion, causing you to delve further into this understanding. This influx of these energies is being felt on earth. And when you have a conscious understanding of what is occurring, it makes it so much sweeter.

When you become increasingly immersed in the Divine Feminine energies, you sense lightness, and Light energies versus the dark energies that have been in existence for so long on your earth. Yes, with both Light and lightness, these energies coincide with your move into love. This gives you a deeper feeling for why you prefer to be gentler, kinder, more nurturing, less apt to anger or engage in drama, and more apt to smile and laugh. These energies are supporting your higher vibrational choices and new ways of being.

I just took a break and saw online a picture of a beautiful rose. Synchronicity continues to validate.

Indeed. And synchronicity comes in waves, does it not? Years ago, you had all those rose synchronicities. Then things quieted, and now a new influx of related signs are revealed just as you are delving into a greater understanding.

The rose is a symbol of who you are at your core. So when you see a rose, you can think of it as a symbol of who you are, a mirror. Is it not true that a rose is often a sign of love given from a spouse or significant other? The rose is given to one's mirror, to celebrate the oneness between them, while it may not be seen in such a deep way. It is a way to look at this symbol now. The rose is you.

Oh Michael, it is now the next morning, and, as you know, one of the last things I set my eyes on before I closed them last night was a picture of a most beautiful white rose. It was one of the most stunning roses I've ever seen. A person posted it on Facebook, and she wrote, "Roses never cease to amaze me." And here, just when I'm about to start my day with you discussing this very subject again, I see a different post online that quotes Rumi: "What was said to the rose that made it open was said to me here in my chest." I will never tire of synchronicity or the beautiful validations you angels provide for us, dearest Michael.

And it gives us great joy to hear that. This is exactly why you are so blessed with synchronicity. You are a superior magnet to it because of your heart

64

connection to it. Ah, yes, the rose symbol is growing in significance. Just as people are intuitively feeling drawn to the sun, they are also drawn to symbols of these times: the rose, the flower of life, certain number combinations, and messages from the skies that are often delivered in symbols. The rose is an important one.

Imagine a rose at the center of your heart. For many incarnations over eons of time, the flower has been closed, but with the promise that one day it will open. And that promise is being delivered now, the rose is blossoming; you are all growing a grand awakening.

When I began to channel messages from you, many times you said that I am a flower about to bloom, and I know you were saying that to us all, as a collective.

It is time to bloom. It is time to reveal to your-selves and the world the true inner beauty of who you are, your souls. Do you see how sweet these times are? With the denser energies of earth, it has been so difficult to get to this core, this beauty. But you are in the midst of evolution, and now is the time to uncover your true essence.

Just now, I realized another synchronicity that occurred during this discussion. Someone who read my book *I Can See Clearly Now* was referring to a passage in it that prompted her own meaningful synchronistic experience, as she described in an email to me. This passage was regarding Anaïs Nin's famous saying: "And the day came when the risk to remain tight in a bud was more painful than the risk it took to blossom." Goodness, Michael, you directed me to that, didn't you? It was an old email, but you led me to go there. I am so grateful for all the validations and emphasis; it helps me to feel your messages more intensely.

Oh my, it is now later in the day, and my son and I just watched the television show *Northern Exposure*. As strange as it may seem to share this in a book of sacred material, every time we watch this show it mirrors something going on in our lives on that very day. Well this time, I was completely overjoyed with the synchronicity. The character, wisdom seeker Chris, said: "Man is born blind. We're little moles, tunneling under the winter rye unaware of the sky above us. We're ignorant folks. It don't matter how many PhDs we've got perma-plaqued on the wall. We're blind and we're ignorant. And there's one piece of information that we don't have. The only piece that will pry open those baby blues, knowledge of self. The answer to all our questions is right here. (He puts his hand over his heart.) Library of Congress. Kabir, Sufi poet, he knew. 'Near your breastbone there's an open flower,' he said. 'Drink the honey that is all around that flower.'"

"Near your breastbone there's an open flower"! I just cannot get over this synchronicity. When you first described in *Michael's Clarion Call* our new way of being—heart centered living—I didn't really see it like I do now. I didn't realize just how rich, complex, and gorgeous this new connection would become. As time goes on and the more I connect with my heart, my rose, my soul, the more I realize the ways that I have ignored the true me. I want to release the old now and grow my authenticity by connecting to my heart.

And that is just it. You are growing your authenticity. It is impossible to be inauthentic when in communion with your heart. Oh the peace that comes with this communion. And this brings me to explaining how the Light, that is increasingly coming through, affects your heart. Your heart is the magnet to this Light. Imagine that, your heart as a magnet to the new Light coming in. Do you see where the feelings of ecstasy would come into play?

Yes, you helped us to understand in *Michael's Clarion Call* that we can actually create feelings of ecstasy; we can literally breathe in ecstasy and experience a taste of Heaven.

So it must be no surprise to you that these feelings are felt in the heart. Give the heart Light and it will dance with joy. It will respond as a mirror to what it is presented with. You are full of potential for great feelings without end. When good things happen, you often expect the bottom to fall out, do you not? With the heart, you will enjoy an increased capacity to attract such good feelings and without interruption in the days to come.

Oh, how sweet it will be. To have a constant supply of Light feeding your heart. It will then become irresistible to live from anywhere but the heart. Truly, this will be a most natural process. Ask your heart about this now.

I hear: "You can live this way much more regularly now. Simply put your attention here and expect great things." Amazing... I then began to feel ecstatic sensations. I am feeling blissed out now. This is incredible. I simply must put into practice making this connection much more regularly than I have been. This makes me tune into my power, and it can be overwhelming, but also incredibly wonderful. The power is within. These may seem like just words to some readers, but they must try this for themselves and trust. We are pioneers in heart-centered living, and I don't want to put off making more intensive, conscious contact with my heart any longer.

I've told you before, you naturally do live from your heart more than you realize. But do you see that all is coming together now to make it easier for you to connect to your hearts. Lessening the complications of your outer life and moving into the simple joys of living are greatly impacting this ability to connect to what is most important.

There has been a natural progression in my life to move away from the material while adopting the feeling that "less is more." Often, I feel increasingly repelled by holding onto things that have little to no meaning. That sounds strong, I know. But I'm not enjoying too much "stuff," as it is often unnecessary. Okay, these feelings of needing to stop being so lazy and releasing more clutter is building in me right now.

Can you imagine what it will be like when things are no longer focused upon like they still are for many? When you live in the higher vibrations, you can attract what you desire so much more easily. And because you do not feel the same attraction to things, you will not feel lack, but rather abundance of all kinds. The need for things will simply lessen, naturally.

*   *   *   *

Michael, you know I need to ask you something. I'm having a heightened awareness of something going on in my reality and you wanted me to bring it up in this forum, so here goes. For some time, I have had memory issues, most notably regarding my short-term memory. I often need to write things down. If I have an appointment somewhere, I must write it down or I will probably miss it. Never before have I experienced this in my life; I used to be much sharper, had good recall, and could hold much more information in my head. On top of this challenge, I feel that I'm only half here, mentally. I don't know where the other half is, but I don't feel fully engaged in this dimension. Even when I am immersed in joy and in the moment, I don't feel fully here to completely enjoy it. This doesn't appear to be due to a lack of being grounded. Although I feel like I'm in between two realities, but I'm not consciously aware of the other one, as strange as that sounds.

It is not strange at all. You are indeed participating in life outside of this dimension, as well. Do you notice how much calmer you are these days? This is because you are anchored in this higher energy and there no fears exist. You've got one step in a higher dimension. We know these times are confusing and strange, and often difficult. But look no further than your heart to charter through these new waters. It's like with your kids who have reached adulthood. Part of them doesn't want to let go of their childhoods and they are in between these realities, charting and navigating through the changes. It is a similar concept.

Well, it can be so frustrating, let alone embarrassing. A couple of days ago, I brought up a subject to a friend, a subject we've broached many times, but I brought it up as if it was a new conversation. She was surprised and said that we had talked about this before, many times. And then suddenly I realized, yes, of course we have. What was I thinking? But throughout the conversation, I felt I was only half there and on autopilot. It was discomforting. Is it because I've moved into my heart even more now which causes my mind's memory to wane?

You have moved into much greater connection with your heart, Mary. Try not to get caught up in all the intricacies of this and just take it at face value. You are shifting, and you are in between two different vibrational realities. Once you fully shift there will be no going back, and I know that you fully celebrate this. You cannot wait for this earth and its occupants to shift, and you often lose patience. When you shift, you will know everything you need to know, so set aside your worries about losing your memory. Just move through these times lightly. You know to laugh your way through and endure the changes with a great sense of humor. Just continue to do so.

PART TWO

Messages from Michael after December 21, 2012

Dearest Michael, it has been some time since we worked on this book. You guided me to set it aside. But it is now just days since the auspicious date of December 21st, 2012, and you are telling me that the time is ripe for more information. I am excited to receive new messages, now with this new energy in place.

And I ask you, do you feel different since this most auspicious date you speak of?

I have to say I do at times feel elevated and excited because I know that something has shifted, but I also have had moments of sadness and frustration. Things still aren't "working" in some important ways. And I'm tired. But then these moments pass and I get excited again.

Yes, and there is nothing strange about your experience. It is not as if everything was to change fully, in but an instant. A recalibration needs to take place as you each align to the changes. And in that experience, one can hold an illusion that things haven't really changed at all. One still doesn't have enough money, one still doesn't feel well, and one is still experiencing third dimensional type frustrations.

I ask you to do just what you are doing. Talk to me when you are frustrated, tune in which always makes you feel better, and keep your energy up. Expend your energy on things that give you joy; focus on that. Say "I am embracing joy in every way I can today." And then you can tone down some of those fluctuations that you speak of.

Well I do love how joy breeds more joy. Yesterday was Christmas, and my son, daughter, and I were just sitting down to open our presents when my girl said, "Oh my God, look at the time! Except it's not really the time!" She was referring to the numbers displayed on our DVR that displays either the time or cable channel. It showed 444! (Again, 444 is known to be the angel's sign of the power of God's love.) I turned on the television and it displayed channel 444, a sports channel. As you know Michael, none of us ever watch sports, nor ever go that high up in the channels. And on top of that, when the television is off, the DVR doesn't display a channel, but rather the time! Even when the tv is on, the DVR displays the channel only temporarily. Oh, how we were so full of joy. It was such a blessing from our angels, to start our special day this way. Was that you?

Indeed it was, along with a chorus of angels present and wishing to surprise you. Whispering to your daughter to notice the numbers, just at the right moment. We delighted in each of your responses. We appreciate your desire to celebrate our gifts to you. You make it most enjoyable for us.

It truly was the icing on the cake of our holiday. To be honest, and as you know, I am just not into Christmas anymore, and I'm referring to the material aspect of it. For the first time ever, we didn't put up our artificial Christmas tree, but rather placed gifts around our indoor palm tree. And we also passed on placing outdoor lights outside, as well. When I sent out Christmas cards, I felt that it would be the last time I would be doing so.

In *Michael's Clarion Call*, you described that we can be in a Christmas state of being every day, regarding the feelings that it provides. So I like to think of it in this way, that we can have Christmas every day. We are moving away from 3rd dimensional, materialistic ways, and I am naturally distancing myself from society's creation of what Christmas is about. And our little 444 miracle yesterday says it all. It was the best part of our Christmas and it was far from material, but rather spiritual.

Yes, why focus on the material when you know where your greatest gifts are? You are simply, as a society, used to the material; but as you say, you are naturally straying. Just as you are naturally straying from certain foods. You can no longer eat low quality "food," or what is called food but really isn't. As I've alluded to before, you have an inner compass that is guiding you, helping you to ease into the changes. And it is a most natural process as long as you get ego and societal demands out of the way.

As I mentioned, these days I'm mostly enjoying a vegetarian diet. Recently, I learned the art of juicing. I choose high quality, organic foods. Yet, I can go off the plan and eat what would be labeled as "junk" quite easily; but it's healthier junk food. Overall, I'm definitely moving in the right direction, just with fluctuations. My new ways of eating leave me feeling content. And I know that many others are following this same path, finding they are naturally drawn to eating more whole live foods. It is fascinating to witness these changes in ourselves and each other!

What else can we expect to naturally shift, without much effort, Michael?

Your ideas. You are blowing the top off of possibilities from what was your 3-D life. You are opening up to new possibilities, things that were not possible before when you as a collective were further from a state of love. As you move further into love, you move further into Divine possibilities and find yourselves creating in new ways. We will talk more about this later.

Also, you are distancing yourselves from mass media and entertainment which continue to reflect the old ways. That is, movies that are violent, news that is distorted and promoting fear, advertising that is clinging onto the old ways promoting products that are on their way out. And there is much more. But you get exactly what I am describing. Many of you can barely stand watching violence of any kind. Your hearts simply cannot take it.

Overall, you are moving from artificial into real. For instance, if you have a choice between riding on a roller coaster, or hiking a beautiful mountain path, more and more are choosing nature's thrills. You are moving from inauthentic to authentic. You are moving into "real-ity." This feeds your soul. Inauthenticity distances you from your soul.

This all resonates perfectly with me. Again, I fluctuate in my habits. For instance, I went months without watching television and perfectly fine without it, but then I suddenly found myself watching it again. The best part of my respite was the break from pharmaceutical commercials. I consider the repetitive watching of and listening to them, which can affect us on subconscious levels, as very unhealthy. While I've never been able to easily watch any kind of violence, that is not an issue. Rather, my desires for that escape into familiar old shows that make me laugh resurfaces and helps me to stay light.

Be easy on yourselves and be in your joy. Simply notice the natural movement and changes and allow for the fluctuations, knowing that you are moving into higher vibrations. Some things are immediate, and others are not.

To be completely honest, I have moments where I can barely stand being here and simply cannot wait for us to shift. As we approached 12/21/12, I fantasized that there would be an immediate halt to violence, from wars and criminal actions, to the sick displays of corruption and untruths in the political arena, media, health industry, etc., which we are constantly subjected to. That the disgraceful and devastating gmos, that are slowly killing us, cease to exist. That the other pollutants in our food, as well as in our skies and water just vanish. That those pharmaceuticals that are dangerous and unnecessary cease to exist, and with it all disease! And the list goes on.

You are closer than you think to seeing such changes. We implore you to keep your eyes on the prize to get you through these final days of mayhem on your earth.

"Keep your eyes on the prize" are words I hold onto, words that you have spoken before. I'm feeling to share the "Diamond Bath" exercise you taught me, which I have led in my presentations and workshops, because it can help us to keep our eyes on where we are headed. And there are also other benefits which you point out. This is what I channeled from you some months ago. I am excited for readers to experience this powerful exercise:

Do you know who you are? You are a human being turning into a human crystalline being. It is time for you to start imagining what you are evolving into. Please close your eyes and perform the exercise after you read the following: *One way you can do this is to imagine yourself lying in a bathtub. Instead of water covering your body, see yourself covered in diamond crystals. Each diamond has an energetic charge that could light up a room. Yet, you have so many around you, hundreds and hundreds of perfectly clear, perfectly cut diamonds charging your beautiful being. Connect to the energy of these beautiful and powerful crystals. Can you feel it? Feel yourself bathing in diamond energy.*

This is a way to raise your frequency, for as you raise your frequency it is much easier to connect and communicate with your angels. When you are feeling low or not worthy of angelic assistance, is it not harder to connect and hear us? I wish for you to take this imaginary bath whenever your intuition tells you to. And when you do, just concentrate on the feelings. Feelings, feelings, feelings... always feel first.

Note: You truly may enter an ecstatic state. My bathtub is quite huge in my imagination. Archangel Michael says that you need not expect this charge to easily dissipate. And when it does, you can always take another bath!

Let me remind readers to find a way to ground this blissful energy deep into their beings. Michael, you once said that keeping ourselves grounded throughout the changes will be a challenge. In *Michael's Clarion Call,* you stated: *This will be your challenge, as you will feel "swept off your feet" in love with the new earth.*

As I explained, for several months I've been feeling as if I am only half here. Even when I am in my joy, I'm not capable of fully being in the moment like I used to be. Again, I do not feel it's an issue of not being grounded, but it could be confused as such. Not that I'm in my past, nor in my future, but I simply don't feel fully here. I bring this up again because my feeling is that I'm far from alone in this experience.

There are many aspects of you, Mary Soliel, as there are of all beings. You are recognizing this now as parts of you venture off and are observing and affecting other realities; basically, you are doing other work. This is partly why you are so tired. Parts of you are doing other things without your conscious awareness and it affects your energy level. It affects your ability to focus and concentrate. We know better than you just how this is affecting you, but we also tell you to not worry. Do not feel there is anything you need other than to go with your heart and accept your expandedness. It is necessary. This is not something to stifle or resist. Acknowledge and accept is what we ask of you.

Do you know you are working with us? There is an aspect of you that is with us at all times. Is this a surprise?

Not really, not when I open my mind up to this news. I so want to be with you, so this actually makes me very happy to know.

You are connected to us through the sound, what you call the "God sound," which you hear in your head at all times now. It connects you to us and you offer your assistance through this connection. You are in communication when you are awake and especially when you sleep, all without being consciously aware, for the most part. And, yet, you know that you are, shall we say, preoccupied?

Well that gives me some understanding. Yes, preoccupied is the word. It also makes me care less and less about the "3Dness" of our world. Since the revelation I shared earlier, that I need to stop being lazy and go through my clutter, I did go through a lot of my belongings and gave away many things. I could do several rounds of this, as it is clear to me that there are things of mine that used to be so meaningful, but just don't have the same meaning anymore. Any pack rat tendencies are leaving me. I can let go of things easier and there is less weighing on this preoccupied mind of mine, lately, in that sense.

My short term memory still has lots to be desired. Well, actually my long term memory does, as well. In a way, I bless it, because it makes me more easily live in the moment, and certainly makes it easier to live from my heart. However, for obvious reasons, it can make everyday living more difficult.

That which you speak of is affecting many souls at this time. This has helped you release the past and fully let go of the third dimensional aspects of you that won't serve you in the higher vibrations. We know of your challenges, and yet things seem to work out somehow, don't they? You know we are helping you, and help everyone who gives us permission to help.

Things do work out. It has not really cost me anything but frustration and embarrassment, at times. On the other hand, it also feels like a huge weight off my shoulders, as memories can tie one down. So I do enjoy that aspect of it. And it has fed my sense of humor.

Speaking of humor, laughing has become an important part of your life, more so now than ever. We love this about you, and we laugh with you often. You are a funny girl.

Well, thank you. My true nature desires to laugh and make others laugh. When I was a young mother, I was so serious about my role, wanting to do all the right things. At one point, I realized I wasn't being a fun mom. Worse yet, I wasn't really being me. Ever since then, I've made it a priority to be fun and make humor a huge part of my life, most certainly with my children.

With the changes we are going through, and with your grand help, I've recognized that laughter is among the greatest gifts that can help us through. And I've attracted people into my life who feel the very same. Lately, I have been laughing more than ever. You have mentioned how laughter raises one's vibration, and so it's no wonder that all of you in the angelic realms laugh so much, existing at such high vibrations.

When you laugh, we laugh. What you may not realize is that not only are you each affecting each other on this planet, but you affect all that is. Including us. Energy begets energy begets energy.

Do you see how the most optimistic, loving, positive people on your planet help not only each other, but all that is, you powerful creators? One day, you will see from a higher vantage point just how this all works. And how negativity and pessimistic attitudes also affect all that is, just as easily. When you understand this, you naturally want to improve your impact.

We say to simply be love. Love is contagious and it is the most powerful force in existence. So when you are simply being love, you are most powerful. Choose to be a channel of love, which is a channel of God. God loves you. God wants nothing more than for you to be in a state of love, which is what He/She is. You can best experience and bring God into your daily conscious life by simply being love.

Oh Michael! I just took a break and went to check in on Facebook, and someone had just posted, "You are a channel of God force energy." This occurred mere seconds after I channeled your words! Synchronicity will never cease to amaze me. Facebook is a powerful arena to witness synchronicity, by the way. On a daily basis, I receive a wealth of synchronistic flow that often helps me to tap into rich understandings and validations. I know that you whispered for me to take a break just so that I would see that post and, thus, affirm this most profound message. Your words about being a channel of God are very touching—I deeply felt the power of those words—and now this synchronicity just propelled me into a state of such joy.

I know that the new Light is helping me to stay in a state of love. But I was surprised that even just yesterday, mere days after December 21, 2012, I slipped into feeling negative about something which then spiraled into not so great of a day.

And then what happened? You recognized where you strayed from love, you immediately analyzed and understood your reaction, cleared yourself, and moved back into love. You know that sometimes you need these reminders, as they often propel you further into love.

Yes, and I forgive myself now. I simply expected things to have changed even more so by now. Just when I thought I've cleared and forgiven, and now we're technically in the beginning of the Golden Age, I got challenged again.

And look at where you are at. You don't even fully recognize many aspects of you now. The challenges will continue as you fully move into this new energy, yet they will also lessen significantly, and they have for you. But on this occasion, you reacted harshly to your own self and took a "tumble." Now you are back on your feet.

Again, there are days it is just so hard to be here. I am sharing this because I know that many relate. As you know, I do believe it is okay and normal to have these feelings. It's not at all a suicidal feeling. It is a "I want to go Home because I cannot stand war and violence and evil and destruction and disrespect for all of life any longer" kind of feeling. But I feel my way back into love every time, because when I move back into this state, I find that love wins. It wins every time. And I know that it doesn't serve to constantly rehash and get upset about what is wrong in this world, when the world is truly changing.

I refer to your words in *Michael's Clarion Call* to gain perspective and recenter: *Focusing on what's wrong with the world, losing hope, taking life for granted, and feeling angry about everything maintains distance from your soul. The choice is yours. And when you go back to the old ways, you can choose again, and again, and again, until love becomes your way.*

A desire to be aware of what is occurring—yet detached while keeping my eyes on the prize—is what feels most helpful. But it truly does seem that just before we are about to be propelled forward, we suddenly can barely tolerate it anymore. Lately, I've noticed this in others, too. They get fed up as well and really feeling the reality that they are actually further distancing themselves from; and then there is some shift that occurs and they feel better about things. They have renewed strength.

Soon, very soon, you won't have those missing Home feelings because you will find yourself ever closer to Home.

*   *   *   *

In recent months, I have felt complete adoration of the sun, obsessed with taking pictures of it, knowing that the New Sun is shining through the sun that we see. I have captured surreal pictures of its rays and colorful orbs extending from it. An example can be seen on the cover of this book, which I photographed when visiting Cathedral Rock, in Sedona, on 11/11/12.

The sun was shining brilliantly all over you during that trip.

Yes, I created four channeled videos while in Sedona, and in three of them, you can definitely see its rays in my face. In the first one, there was a distinct magenta-colored light coming through, which I've never seen before. What was that?

That was a symbol of my love for you. For you were spreading your light and my messages, and that was a tremendous gift. So that was my gift to you. That was my way of saying "thank you."

I am deeply touched, Michael. While I hadn't asked you what that was about, I think you wanted me to bring it up here, to make the point that our angels gift us in innumerable and miraculous ways. I will keep this in the book, but not in a way that says: "Oh look at what Michael did for me, how special I am," but rather "Look at what our angels can do to show their love for us." I know I'm no more special than anyone else. I just feel strongly to make that point again. We all have the same ability and right to have a relationship with our angels, archangels, ascended masters, and guides.

This is true. Do you notice that even when you are speaking in your own voice, I am helping you to express what I know you wish to express?

Yes, I do. And I most certainly need and appreciate your help. After I wrote *I Can See Clearly Now,* a book that was not consciously channeled, I realized that you were helping me tremendously "behind the scenes," and without my awareness, for the most part. Certainly, you and the angels were behind many of the synchronicities that occurred while writing it, and which I identified throughout the book.

Just as I articulated in a recent videotaped message of mine, I really don't know where I stop and you start when I do my work. And this is becoming increasingly so. I no longer close my eyes when I channel for my videotaped messages, and I almost feel that we are heading into new territory together; regarding the messages coming from us as a team.

This is hard for me to share because I don't want to come across as grandiose here. But suddenly, everything is coming together, feelings I've had but have not truly spoken. You want us to come through even more so as a team. Because this will symbolize how we are at one with our angels! I have chills right now. I'm getting this, Michael.

I wish to share with readers that my friend, singer/songwriter Mia Mantello, wrote a song about Michael and me, called "Michael and Mary." She and her musician friends performed it prior to one of my presentations in Maine. It was and will forever be an immense honor. It is now on her new CD "The Flower in Your Heart." Around this time, Mia also asked her friend Marianne Swittlinger to make me an amulet, which she did, and because Marianne saw me present in Maine, this kind woman wouldn't accept money and rather insisted on creating this for me as a love offering. I felt such love coming my way from these beautiful people. When I received it in the mail on Christmas Eve, I was so very touched. On one side of the beading spells the name "Michael"—when you move the beads appropriately—and on the other side, "Mary."

These gestures, even more than beautifully symbolizing our bond, are helping me to recognize what I believe you are whispering to me, that it is time to take the next step. You wish for me to use this as an example for us all. That when we partner with the angels, we become a team and we should not see ourselves as separate. We should not see ourselves as lower. We are all aspects of God and we can allow our angels to meet us in this state of oneness, rather than separateness. We just are not trained to think and be this way, but this will change. Okay, now I really have chills with this understanding.

Synchronicity has really aided in this under-standing. You were having this feeling during your last message (a youtube video created for the powerful day of 12/21/12), *which you thought was going to be a channeled message. But rather you just spoke on your own and yet you knew that I was with you. I wished for you to do so. And you are so completely right. This is how it shall be now... Messages from Michael and Mary. The song, the gift, are all Divinely underscoring our bond and the new way of seeing our partnership. As one.*

I am honored more than ever before. My task will be to not fear how this could be viewed—as egocentric or illusory—and to dispel fears of people wondering, "Who is she to elevate herself to that level?" Because, as always, I know that you wish for me to be the messenger. And that I must walk the talk of the messages in this book, as best as I can. Our work together will be as a team, like never before. Messages from Michael and Mary.

This was all part of the plan. You indeed have it right. And from this point on our messages in this book shall come through as one...

PART THREE

Messages from Michael and Mary

It is time to drop any misbeliefs about who you are, reader. You are a source of Divine love. And you are worthy of miracles that mirror exactly who you are. Are you ready to own your magnificence? Are you ready to allow miracles into your daily life?

Imagine yourself standing, but several feet taller than you are. Imagine Light emanating from your being and you see yourself as beautiful. Feel it, feel the Light coming from the New Sun, through your being and then radiating outward touching one another. Touching the earth. Touching all the vibra-

tional levels of, and beings in, the Heavenly realms. You are youthful and glowing. You have all the energy you need. And you are aware of your powerful creating skills. This is who you really are... behind the façade of the human mask.

This is the new human. The new human that you are becoming. We treasure the transformation in each of you. From caterpillar to butterfly, you are moving into a freedom that is beyond what you have ever imagined.

Embrace with joy and excitement the following changes that provide a glimpse of both what is occurring and what is to come:

1. ***Lightness of being.*** *You will become lighter in all ways. You will be lighter in a physical way. Your thoughts will be lighter; no longer mired in third dimensional concerns and mental traps of the ego. You will feel lighter, emotionally, because you will be living from the heart where your greatest wisdom lies, and where fear does not exist. You will speak lighter, meaning you will no longer find reason to speak in anger, or fear, or anything that lowers the self and the receiver, but rather speak in ways that exude love and respect. Your experiences will be lighter as you will no longer experience shock and have deeper understanding of your daily occurrences.*

2. ***Heart centered living.*** *You will experience fully a new way of being, and it is all created from living from the heart. Heart-centered living completely changes the paradigm that you know now. War, corruption, greed, hatred,*

bullying, discrimination, judgment, jealousy, et cetera, cannot exist when living from the heart. You will see yourself and others as who you really are, and disrespect for the human can no longer occur in the new energy.

3. ***Choices of sustenance.*** *Your choices in physical nourishment will continue to evolve toward plant-based choices as eating animal flesh will, eventually, no longer be tolerated by the new human body. Pseudo foods that presently claim to be food will no longer be available or desired as their synthetic, poisonous ingredients cannot exist in the higher vibrations. By this we are referring to many types of "foods" you would find in packages, cans, and drive-through restaurants, for instance. It will be a natural change because as you grow your vibrations, you also grow your resistance to anything that no longer matches those vibrations. And eventually, there will come a time when humans will no longer need food, as the Light from the New Sun becomes their sole source of energy.*

4. ***The accessing of memories lessen.*** *When you are in the higher vibrations, you no longer desire to access memories like you do now. You can use memories as a crutch to make you feel better about a situation. To think back to a happier time, perhaps. But in this new energy, you are more in the moment and are creating everything you desire. There will be a lessened need to be outside of the present moment.*

5. ***Loving your body.*** *You will love your physical body, no matter how you may feel*

about your body now. You will one day feel as if you have drunk from the fountain of youth. You will be able to recreate your physical body with so much ease, unlike in the third dimension. And because you are being love, you recognize the love that you are, and you accept your physical selves completely. So much of your physical looks are a result of so many influences experienced as a 3-D human: past lives, misbeliefs, disease and lack of good health, et cetera. Imagine when these influences no longer touch you, and you appear as a reflection of who you really are.

6. ***Living in your passion.*** *Whatever you desire, you can attain in the higher vibrations. You will have unlimited freedom to pursue new opportunities, new creations, and new sources of enjoyment when you live in your passion. You may completely switch gears in what you do in the new energy, and how you serve others and yourself in the new world. You will find talents and abilities that were locked deep inside your being, suddenly surface. You will explore the possibilities and find complete freedom to pursue your greatest passions.*

7. ***Your senses fully awaken.*** *You will have greater abilities to tap into your senses, finding that you can see and hear differently, in more metaphysical ways. Touch will feel different as well. Your psychic sense will sky-rocket. All your senses will be affected. And you will grow your connection to your senses,*

and, thus, live with greater physical aware-
ness in this new world.

8. ***Your feelings will rule.*** *Your choices,*
reactions, and experiences will all be feeling
based... feelings first. Because you will become
powerful conscious creators, you do this by
connecting to the feelings in your heart. Life
will feel so different, and you will respond to
the changes from the aspect of feelings, not
thinking. You will connect to all beings, all
stimuli, all experiences directly from your
heart. For those who may be emotionally de-
tached and cannot easily express themselves,
known to be a more male quality—but exper-
ienced in both males and females—you are
moving into more feminine energies and will
embrace the connection to your emotions.
Imagine the New Sun's Light swelling in your
heart and you project that Light outward.
This is a good image to behold.

9. ***Magic and miracles are widespread and***
constant. *You will be connected to the magic*
and miracles the Universe provides, but
without judgment or disbelief. You will never
for a moment be bored in your new life. You
will experience a great rise in witnessing new
phenomena and manifestations that will thrill
you. Just as you're starting to see changes in
the sky that are astounding some of you, you
will see all aspects of life at higher vibrations.
We speak of auras and angels, for example.
And seeing what was unseen to most, in the
third dimension. You will feel as if you are in
a dream. But will soon find that you had been

living a dream, and now moving into reality.

10. **Freedom of movement.** *You will one day in the future move as the angels do. If you truly create Heaven on earth, you need to realize that you will adopt aspects of this realm into your life, but as an elevated human being. So this means you will one day be able to teleport. And in some future time will no longer need the transportation vehicles you have now. You will enjoy this lightness of being also, a grand gift in your evolution.*

11. **Creativity will be abundant in all aspects of daily living.** *You will paint your new lives with creativity as the driving force. Creativity has been stifled in your children as they grow, and, certainly, as adults. But as you live as an enlightened being, you naturally access your creative skills. You become more child-like as you embrace the creative side of things. You will see the world with new eyes, like a child does, except it really is a new world to see! And, most importantly, you learn how to become master creators, which requires creative envisioning.*

12. **You live among the angels.** *Well, you already do, all the time. You are constantly in the presence of angels and guides, but you will consciously live among us. One day, you will see us. Until then, your senses will increase your understanding of connection with us. You are already starting to feel our touch, perhaps see a spark of light, or notice the orbs. You delight in the signs we send you, as you acknowledge how we use synchronicity to*

connect with you, as well as gift you. This will grow in all ways until one day, we will all be in conscious connection with each other; and this includes passed loved ones, as you approach the end of grief—a third dimensional emotion.

13. **Your navigating skills take a quantum leap.** *We're not talking about your ability to read a map, although you can throw that in the mix. We want you to know that you will have a greatly strengthened ability to navigate your own life from your heart: how to live it, what to do, where to go, who to connect with— all that serves your highest good.*

14. **Your heart will open to others like never before.** *By this we mean that the predominant "me" way of being will naturally transform to a "we" way of being. You understand the interconnectedness not just between humans, but all beings and all of nature. Your heart will embrace life in all its forms and you will feel in love with the earth and all living things. It will feel ecstatic.*

15. **You will feel true ecstasy.** *We in the Heavenly realms are in bliss. We reside at a high vibration that is actually ecstatic; it is our natural state. And you, as fifth dimensional humans, will also live in an ecstatic state. Are you understanding how war and violence can never occur again on your earth? You will only know love and joy, and there will be no need to endure the negative emotions and beliefs that can translate into the most negative actions known to man. In fact,*

it will be impossible. Sexual energy—specifically, the orgasmic climax—best describes how you will feel in this ecstatic state, but you will feel it throughout your whole being. When one reaches a climactic state, is it possible to hold a negative or sad thought at the same time? It is impossible. Sexual relations will be grander, and the act of sex will become sacred once again.

16. **Everyday stressors will be nonexistent.** *Worries about money, physical appearance, lack of possessions, et cetera, will cease to exist in the new energy. Imagine how much lighter you will feel from that alone. Stress, a great trigger of poor health and unhappiness, will cease to exist. Think of it as if being on the best vacation of your dreams, but it never ends. You are slowly starting to see some stresses ease. Partly because you are lessening your attention toward them as you move into more simplified, and, yet, richer lives.*

17. **You recognize God in you.** *The piece of God that lies in every human being will unveil itself and grow in significant ways. You will become more God-like and will embrace your spiritual side more than a hundredfold. You will not be living in your pasts any longer, but if you were to examine them, you would be shocked at how you ever got to live so distant from God in the first place. But all of that societal programming will leave you. You will march to your own drummer, and hand in hand with God.*

18. ***You will have perfect health.*** *With your cells and DNA changing, and the constant influx of Liquid Light, you will one day have perfect health and it will be impossible for your body to hold disease, just as it is for us in the angelic realms. One cannot live in the higher dimensions and be in such imbalance, that one would carry disease. Genetics, stress, unsound choices, environmental influences, et cetera—these determining factors will no longer be of concern.*

19. ***The end of mental chatter.*** *That chatter, often a product of negative thoughts and worries, will no longer exist. The mind will no longer drive you. As you know now, your heart will. And you cannot have heart chatter. What comes from your heart is all relevant, it is pure, and it is of the highest vibrations. Mental chatter is part of the equation of how you create what you don't want in your life. You have a thought, and it can go into endless chatter which exacerbates the energy of just what you don't want. Do you see how this absence of unsupportive thoughts also lends to your creative futures?*

20. ***Technology on the rise.*** *So many changes in technology will astound you. You are on the brink of great discoveries, as well as the resurfacing of old, revolutionary discoveries previously hidden from the world but to be exposed and utilized. There will be change, change, and more change to make the world easier to live in. The biggest difference will be that your spiritual level will be a match to*

your technological level. Whereas, in the past, technology and your world weren't best served when in the hands of those who were spiritually disconnected.

21. **You will see each other as equals.** *Everyone will be recognized for who they really are. And in that recognition, it will be understood that no soul is greater than another. The past ways of idolizing and revering the relatively few among you will no longer occur as you see and respect the full magnificence of every being.*

22. **You will create from your conscious mind.** *You will no longer be tied to your subconscious mind. You have all been, to a great degree, creating your lives from your subconscious minds which hold beliefs and scripts molded from your pasts—meaning your childhoods, especially, as well as your past lives. In the coming days, you will increasingly see yourself creating from outside of this paradigm, and it will be most freeing. This is what you have been waiting for.*

23. **You will see life from a galactic viewpoint.** *Rather than viewing yourself and your surroundings as a citizen of just your locality, country, and even world, you will have a galactic understanding of who you are and how you are connected to all that is. You will connect to other star systems, other beings from beyond what you presently know or have experienced. When we say you are not separate, we truly mean that you are not separate*

from any thing or place or being... you are truly connected to all that is.

These changes represent only part of what is ahead. Again, as expressed in this book and in Michael's Clarion Call, *your minds cannot fully comprehend all that is coming your way. Simply because so much of it is out of mind; it is outside of any experience or understanding you have ever had. We hope this gives you excitement and drive to move forward with much determination. You are indeed pioneers discovering this new world.*

The new earth will not disappoint. You will not miss the old ways. Rather, you will embrace each Divine change since fear will no longer be "in the picture."

How can you prepare for these changes, to help make your transition with more ease?

Breathe. *Breathe consciously, as often as you can. Tune into your breath and with the intake, breathe in the comfort and support of God's love. And breathe out anything that is not supporting you in the moment, such as fear or negative thoughts. Just breathe in God, again and again. It will fill you with a great sense of unconditional love and peace. It can even send you into a state of ecstasy. Just take whatever comes.*

Live from the heart. *Get used to the new way of being, where your heart runs you, not your mind. Where the highest emotion of love runs you, not fear or any of its counterparts. Oh, how glorious this way of living will be. You will know what true, authentic joy is. And when gathered with others, it will mul-*

97

tiply. When you travel alone, it's difficult because you want to share the new sights with another. The same will occur with your movement into love. You will want to share the new feelings with another.

Be out in nature. *We know you hear this so often. And that is because nature is beckoning you, it is speaking to you often to get outside of your homes and connect. Sure, you can connect while inside your home, with your imagination. But there is nothing like being out in nature, and accessing all of its gifts. So much goes unseen while in nature. There is an energy exchange you may be completely unaware of. And let us ask you this. Do you normally come home from a walk, a hike, a swim, or some experience outdoors feeling sad or upset? Make the connection of how good you feel after your visit. And bring nature into your home as much as you can, whether it be a plant, a rock, a water feature, or a flower. Increase your connections; make it a priority to be outside in the sun, under the telling skies, and it will more than rejuvenate you.*

Honor your past self. *By this we mean, honor the old you that got you to the new you. Honor all that you endured and experienced which brought you to this point in time, your graduation. All of it was crucial, what you would deem "good" or "bad," simply because it brought you to this point of no return. Release any last bits of guilt and resentment toward yourself, as well as others.*

Throw love on everything. *As you continue to go through challenges and frustrations, simply throw love on all those things you encounter that simply require love. Do this in whatever way feels right and comes naturally to you. Whether it be speaking and* feeling the words "I throw love on (the issue)," holding a vision of dropping bundles of love all over it, or whatever feels good. It is a practice filled with great energy.

Let go of the concept of lack. As you move toward higher vibrational living, you release your grip on lack and "not enough-ness." You find yourself creating a life filled with contentedness and completeness. One day, lack will never again be part of your experience. We know that this sounds too good to be true. But that is a result of your third dimensional experiences, and beliefs that are naturally formed from that level of living.

Talk to your angels. If you haven't begun communicating with your angels, this is a great time to do so. We are fully committed to ensuring your arrival into your new world, with as much ease and understanding as possible. You can make the job of the angels much easier and gain from their gifts, simply by bringing them into your world and your daily life. Since you have free will, you must give us permission to interfere, to help you with your problems. But once you do that, you open yourself to being adorned with limitless possibilities in how we can make a difference in your lives.

Trust God. God knows what He/She is doing! And part of God exists in you. So put your faith on that which you can fully count on, most especially when you are feeling overwhelmed or saddened by the present difficulties that continue to occur on earth.

Release the third dimensional aspects of your world. Many of you have opened your eyes to the insanity that has plagued your planet for eons of *time. The killing of another, whether it is through war, a violent rampage, or a slow killing through poisoned foods or irresponsible pharmaceuticals, for example—this is true madness. You've increasingly felt the need to label it as such because your eyes have opened to the reality of what all humans and their tender spirits have endured for so long now. Move past the ugliness through the promise of change before you. The promise that evil will never again descend on your earth. Greet the evolution of the human, of your very own self, with open arms.*

Release the third dimensional aspects of you. *As you have been forced to confront and move through the last of your karma, you have thus confronted what no longer serves the evolving being that you are. Those third dimensional parts of the human personality that may include judgment, hatred, prejudice, jealousy, anger, et cetera, are in the midst of leaving.*

Avoid negative and difficult connections. *Wherever possible, distance yourself energetically, and with love, from those still clinging to the old ways. Even when in their company, you can protect your energy with your intention, but it's best to limit these interactions. You can only shine your Light and be you, but you cannot force another to change. Constant interactions with those choosing fear over love can hold you back. Seek out those who emit like energy, who nourish your spirit rather than causing harm or setbacks.*

Part Four

Questions for Michael

At this point, Michael, I understand that it is appropriate to communicate separate from you, and ask you some important questions. Even though these questions come from me, I feel they may be representative of questions from many whose eyes are reading these words. At the very least, it may interest them.

1. I can hear your answer before I ask this one, but when exactly will we be firmly rooted in the fifth dimension? Some believed it would occur on December 21, 2012.

There is no answer to this question yet. Aside from what you may hear from channels and prophets, this date is not set in stone. It will be revealed to you when things truly are set in stone, so to speak. But within eight years of your time (by 2021), life on this planet will indeed be very different.

2. As my heart and soul desire simplicity and ease, I'm finding it increasingly difficult to tend to day-to-day complications, such as house issues, dealing with company services, business related responsibilities, etc. Part of me just wants to move somewhere remote, where daily living comes easy and much less complicated so that I can focus solely on my spirituality and work. How can I better cope with my feelings and responsibilities?

When you removed clutter and things you no longer need in your home, you were barely paying attention to your decisions, just seeming glad to be rid of things. You are naturally handling this challenge better than you think. You see, you have somewhat divorced yourself from the complexities of day-to-day living. So while you know you must tend to your responsibilities, you do so but with a detachment you have never demonstrated before. You are going through the necessary motions, but with much more emotional detachment. For instance, you have always disliked the process of preparing taxes, but the last time you did them, you did so with the greatest ease you've ever experienced with this process, simply because you emotionally detached and just went through the necessary motions in this way. This is the secret... detach and conquer quickly, and continue to seek and embrace simplicity.

3.   My friend, Lee, recently wrote me saying, "The sky seems so much more *vast*, and the sun is white now, not yellow." He also mentioned how much brighter the sun appears to be. I've noticed the same. Just yesterday, it felt as if my sunglasses couldn't provide enough protection to help me see in such brightness! The sun appears larger on some days. The skies are lighter in color, as it seems increasingly rare to see a deeper blue-colored sky (although I assume that has to do, at least partly, with chemicals being sprayed in the sky). Can you explain in greater depth what we are sensing here?

Here is another example of how it may only appear that things are the same, to most people, but they really aren't. The New Sun is transforming the effects and presence of the sun that you have known as third dimensional beings. It's as if there is this new metaphysical template in the sky, and with the veil thinning, we are utilizing a closer connection with you now, via your very skies. The New Sun makes this possible. Think of it this way: with the creation of this new template, it allows us to work in a synergistic way with you and connect with you, such as through the magical clouds you are now seeing, with faces "painted" on them. Mary, you do think of us as painting your skies, and that is certainly a way to look at it. We are expressing ourselves through the sky as if it were a canvas. And yes, with your sun being the entryway to allow the New Sun to come through, this creates all new dynamics, with the pairing of energies with the sun you are familiar with.

4. Since December 21, 2012, many of us are noticing palpable changes, exciting changes, and those of us who have felt stuck are now breaking through with sudden opportunities, ideas, and support coming out of the wood-work. While this is more than welcomed, it can also be overwhelming. Do you have any advice? I know I am one of those feeling somewhat overwhelmed.

   You are entering into a time of increased manifestation capabilities. So as you put your thoughts out, the appropriate response from the Universe is swifter and more profound. This alone can be overwhelming, in addition to the actual projects or opportunities that may be courting you.

   If you feel the pull to work on something, work on it. But trust your heart to navigate the timing. Go by your heart's schedule, not a date you put in your "day-timer." Reassess your goals through your heart, and you will find much greater clarity. This is one example of how you are lessening your reliance on third dimensional constructs.

You suggested that I go meditate now, and I had the most amazing experience. I don't know how else to describe this other than saying that I believe I just time traveled. While I was in a sleepy state, I was aware of who and where I was. But suddenly, I found myself in my beloved grandparents' home, standing on this landing they had at the side of their house once you walked in. Just a few steps up and to the right was the kitchen where my grandmother spent most of her time cooking incredible meals for us. I just told a friend that my grandma once said the most touching words to me when I was a young girl; it was casual and unexpected, and we were standing on this very landing. Anyways, I looked around and everything was familiar; the smells, the walls, the flooring, and the layout. I then saw two different wall hangings, which I had completely forgotten about, and yet there they were in perfect detail. It made me feel very emotional. This was proving to me that I was in a past reality and at the moment I walked up the steps and cried out for my dear grandmother, I just snapped out of it, but with full recall. What is happening?

Note: My intuitively gifted friend Cindy shared that she had something like this occur with her. In her case, she found herself in her old high school. She described that it felt as if there was no time, and it was quite fleeting without a specific experience; she was just simply

105

there. I realized that in both of these situations, we were going back to happy times, times that hold very positive memories.

You are getting glimpses of no time. Time was no barrier in your ability to be a participant in a reality of your past. Because this place was a very special place in your heart, and it provided you with a profound memory, your soul actually took you there. You will continue to receive glimpses like this, and as you can see, it did not jar you, but rather excited you. As you know, there is reason for everything. When you raise your vibrations, the reasons increase, everything becomes more illuminated, and the Light of the New Sun brings greater profundity to your ever evolving existence.

As I process this, I am realizing it can be likened to the movie *It's a Wonderful Life*, where Jimmy Stewart's character was taken to different places on his timeline by an angel. It helps to associate with something familiar to us—even if it's merely from a fictional movie—in order to define it. The strange thing is that instead of the experience sending me off into the clouds, I feel quite grounded, and this happened less than an hour ago.

This experience has set a new tone of excitement in your present journey, and it creates a new level of expectation and anticipation that places you firmly into your body and ready for the next adventure. You are wanting this shift of the ages with all your heart and soul, so every new experience is grounding you into your changing and growing reality. Such as your excitement when you see miracles in the skies. However, if you couldn't embrace or attach an understanding to the experience, you would not be feeling so grounded.

5. All levels of our being are changing so much. Regarding what many commonly refer to as "Ascension Symptoms"—side effects of our changing physical, mental, emotional, and spiritual bodies—they seem to be much more pronounced since 12/21/12. They are affecting our sleep, our eating habits, our emotions, our relationships, our physical bodies, etc., in so many ways. Is this true, and why is it so? (You can search "Ascension Symptoms" on Google.com if you wish to learn more.)

    While everyone isn't experiencing the same symptoms of change nor at the same time, you are each going through a tremendous inner metamorphosis. And it is building in you now as change, in general, is speeding up. Breathe through the changes and you will actually find gifts in them. Many of you do not like that your sleeping time has been reduced, but are you not sometimes getting more accomplished in a given day? Or you find much frustration over your lack of focus, but have you not enjoyed a break in, perhaps, too many activities which led you to prioritize them which has thus better served you? Seek the gifts in this metamorphosis you are exper-

iencing and you will ride through the changes more quickly and easily. Be less reactive and, rather, surrender to the process.

6. Many of us continue to feel poverty consciousness created from our past (possibly in this life and, especially, in past lives) which still resides in our subconscious, and haven't quite broke out of this and into the new, growing reality of abundance for all. How can you help us turn this tide?

    When you shift into new territory, each time there are lingering effects of the "old." One day, you are feeling confident and excited about your present situation and hope for your future, and then the next day you find yourself feeling the extreme opposite—lacking abundance, which can then create fear. Be patient. You are in the most supportive energies now, unlike any in all of your lifetimes. Revel in every success, every sign, and do so with your brothers and sisters, as well. Share in each others' successes and miracles and keep your eyes on your greatest desires. Talk to us and let us help you out of your limiting thoughts. We are your cheerleaders, devoted towards helping you to manifest the magnificence that mirrors who you are. And who you are is not of lack in any way, whatsoever. This goes for each and every one of you. When you are who you really are, you are God-realized; and God is abundant, forevermore.

7.   I care about my friends and acquaintances very much, as you know. However, I'm feeling so overwhelmed hearing about others' problems, especially lately. It is making me distance myself to preserve my energy, especially so that I can do my work.

While your work attracts those seeking help, and you experience this more than the average being, you know you are not alone in this frustration. This is why we ask each of you to go within and work with us for your greatest help. Of course, you can go to each other to share and help get through your challenges, but when it gets excessive, it impedes another's energy greatly. Balance is necessary in all things and, most especially, through these changing times. Also, simplifying your life will ease the weight of your emotional and mental pressures, significantly.

8.   What I am about to describe is what people could consider "woo woo." But I'm not going to pretend that this didn't happen. In fact, it actually thrills me.

Yesterday, I went grocery shopping. Before I got out of the car, this random thought occurred to me that there is a penny right outside my car door—I felt sure of it. But when I opened the door and scanned the area, there was no penny. I went shopping, and when I returned to the car, lo and behold there was a penny on the ground, right next to my car door. But that's just a little story compared to what happened next.

I returned home, and went around my car to the passenger side where I had two canvas bags filled with groceries and my cell phone (which is always at the ready now, in order to stop and take cloud pictures) sitting on the front passenger seat. My purse was on the car floor. When I first picked up the phone, it was as if it were knocked out of my hand, flew up an inch or so and then disappeared from view! Did it go into either bag of groceries? It wasn't in the bag closest to it—neither bag, in fact. It must have fallen under the seat. But the phone was nowhere to be seen. I took the grocery items out of each bag, but again, no phone anywhere. It couldn't have flown into my closed purse, which was about a full foot away. So I took the groceries into the house and went through everything again. When I couldn't find it, I went back to look in the car again. I was completely baffled. Once back inside my home, I said to myself that I'll check inside my purse but there is no way it could be in there as it was closed and too far away. But there it *was*! There is no logical explanation for this. I know that someone from another realm was having fun with me! Was it you, Michael?

Would you be surprised if it were?

No, not at all.

Well it certainly was. I'm glad you are smiling now. We knew you would be pleased at what you labeled "woo woo." We know that you are aware of the possibilities and can

*easily accept that a being from another di-
mension had a hand in this. I wanted to show
you again how we can influence matter. The
penny, the phone, and the other experiences
you had, including with your gold cross (as
described in I Can See Clearly Now) and the
bald eagle, have all shown you the same
thing—we can and do make things appear,
disappear, and reappear. Would you believe
that it is now an easier process for us? With
the dimensions growing closer together, we
are able to have a greater affect on your
physical plane; whether we are affecting the
clouds or affecting any type of matter. So this
was another preview that I wished for you to
share.*

PART FIVE

Special Messages from the Heavens

There are several beings who wish to impart a message here. They are excited to share such good news.

Mary Magdalene

Yes, it is I, Mary Magdalene. Mary, you feel a connection to me, you always have. As well as many of you whose eyes are on this page, and I tell you... Before you came here, in this particular incarnation, I spoke to you of the potential changes that would occur, to prepare you for just what you are going through now. But then, as you become human, the blinders go on, and you forget who you really are, and you, perhaps, forget our connection. Yet we are all connected and for always. So, in this message, I wish to remind you of several things. You were brought here on purpose, and for a mighty purpose, to bring forth this Golden Age. You knew it would not be easy, but there would be no greater experience as a human. You might say it's your greatest soul assignment. And here you are now, on the threshold of such great change. We have asked you in so many ways, through so many messengers, to connect with us so that we can help you through. If you wish to have a conscious connection with me, simply call on me and know I am with you. As your world moves into the gentler and softer energies that I have spoken of, also referred to as the Divine Feminine energies, you will know a peace that you have never known as a human. The emotion of fear is slowly melting away as love dominates your planet. Go into your heart now and feel my connection to you there. Feel my love and appreciation for you, for your role in bringing forth the evolution of a planet and its inhabitants. Can you feel me in your heart? Listen to my whispers. I love you. I want you to know that your courage and determination are known to us all. We are your biggest cheerleaders. We celebrate your every accomplishment. And we hold you during your trying times. Do not overly concern yourself with what is going to happen when. It is impossible for you to understand exactly what life will be like, so just relish all the positive changes you are witnessing and know that everything will unfold just as it should. Simply hold onto the promise of a love filled earth. And in that promise, be in peace, dear ones.

Jesus
I made a promise to you when I was on earth, and now it is coming to fruition. You are moving toward becoming the enlightened and advanced human that I promised you would be. You are becoming who you really are, and from that place you will create miracles and venture into new territories that are beyond what your mind can now entertain. When you look back on your life, you will become aware of how things were perfectly set up to bring you to this point. You, as a collective, had moved so far from God and the true understanding of your spirituality, so that you could now see what has been lacking and fully embrace it. Extremes are often necessary for understanding and, thus, your growth and change. Your spirituality is now your priority. Many of you chose material things as your priority, a relationship with another as your priority, or your work as your priority; but you are now seeing your Divine self as the priority. You are awakening to your blossoming spirit. And your spirit outshines everything that your third dimensional world provided. The human race simply forgot. But now they are remembering. Their very souls are reaching out and making their true selves known. Just imagine what this will look like. And simply sit in the wonderment of what is to come.

Chamuel
I am here to speak of love, of romantic love which most of you have or desire as human beings. Love relationships are changing, changing indeed.

Whereas relationships, in many cases, cease to last as long as the couple may intend, or cause too much pain and unhappiness, it is because relationships for the most part have been serving the personality—the third dimensional aspects of each being—and not the soul. The further you are from your soul, the more challenges a couple will face. However, when you learn to live from your heart, and express your soul, you attract the best relationships for you on the deepest of levels. This cannot help but bring to you the most solid and meaningful relationships. Love breeds love, and when you tap into the love that you are, you can attract another who resonates to the true you. And ecstasy is then yours. As you move further into who you are, some relationships continue to work well and some can no longer continue in your daily reality. If the latter is your experience, and the parting of ways is necessary, do your best to part in love, and not anger and resentment. If one partner is unhappy, it is not a healthy situation for either. You do not know what or who is around the corner. Have faith and be at peace, always seeing the higher picture. Know that these are times of great changes, and holding onto the familiar, when it is not serving you, will hamper the flow to your own true happiness. When you are connected to your soul, you will attract the right person to you. Often it will seem as if by magic. The Universe is a powerful match-maker and truly can and does make meetings happen!

Quan Yin

Oh my love for you, all of you, is overflowing. I am committed to overseeing your movement into love, for love is everything. You are love and I love you. I love you without condition. You cannot even understand the love I have for you, that we all do. It is a higher love that extends from all that is through us and to you. It is like a beam of Light flowing to you that is a more powerful force than anything on your earth. Think of love in this way. The most powerful force. Thinking that anything else is more powerful is merely an illusion. Things are playing out on your earth, that illusively take you away from love, but love is winning. Because love is truth, and fear and all of the low vibrational aspects of your existence up until now are false and falling away. All the parts of you that aren't grounded in love are also falling away. You've been in a long waiting period, a deep hibernation, and you are getting ready to fully awaken. Do not expect things to remain the same. If you are still mired in holding onto the familiar, it is time to reason out what is truly going on, see things from a higher perspective, and learn to embrace the changes leading you out of this dream you've been in for so long. The dream has inflicted much pain on your soul. Imagine a wave of love washing away this pain, pain over eons of time, and giving you a fresh new start. Does that sound worthwhile? Does that sound worthy of letting go of the old? The old ways are never to "work" again. You are entering into new territory that will deliver a greater health and wealth than you have ever experienced as a human.

Archangel Gabriel

I wish to cover the topic of laughter. I realize that this may surprise you. But laughter is an immediate cleanser of your pain. To laugh is to bring forth heightened joy into your energy field. This channel was in a movie theater with her son and daughter yesterday. She broke into laughter about something she found very funny, even though the movie was a serious one. And it got contagious with her children, so she had to move to a different seat several rows down from where they were sitting in order to finish watching the movie without disturbing others. Outside of the stressful aspect of her experience, she felt a huge clearing of stuck energy within her, and she knows exactly what I'm talking about, even though she didn't expect me to broach this topic! So I ask you to allow yourself to enjoy the act of laughing as it is one of the most enjoyable activities for humans, as well as all of us in the angelic realms. And it will help you to lighten your difficulties, now more than ever. Laughter keeps you in your heart, so allow yourself to let go and just feel the joy of it.

Mother Mary

Oh beloved humans moving so quickly on the continuum to great change. Can you muster up the courage to seek your highest truth, your greatest expression, your best dream realized? You do this by becoming an authentic human. You no longer hide behind a façade, a mask of who you are. It is time to take off the mask. It is time to live in your truth and realize, experience, and fully own your magnificence. Imagine doing this now. You have been wearing a mask, perhaps without knowing it. Your concerns of what society, strangers, and even loved ones judging you or trying to hold you back are lessening now. Release the shackles that have suppressed you, and set yourself free. Ask your heart what it is you need to do and know in order to become a full expression of who you are. When you follow your heart, you can never, ever go wrong. You cannot hold fear if you are truly in your heart. So learn to trust and make best friends with your heart. Move with your heart every day. Speak with your heart. Act with your heart. Be one with your heart in all ways. Your courage will be instantaneous when you have true connection. You won't settle for less, only what is in agreement with your soul. Take small steps if you wish. Just ask what is in your highest interests to do in any given moment? Is it to rest your body? Is it to connect with someone? Is it to soften an angry feeling you just had? Is it to perform an act of loving kindness? Is it to turn off the television? Is it to support another? Is it to celebrate an accomplishment you had today? Is it to immerse yourself in some project that you've been dreaming of? Is it to choose differently when it comes to food? Is it to take a gentle, but powerful, stand for yourself? Start there, get used to this connection, and it will grow into the most natural process.

Archangel Ariel

Can you believe what is occurring now on your beloved earth—all of the changes? Are your eyes wide open to it? May it be so. This is no time to put your head in the sand. If you do so, you will experience shock and fear, whereas if you stay on top of the changes, you will experience understanding and peace, no matter what is occurring. Throw in excitement about your new life that is forming, and you are making the most of this experience, and will better sail through the changes. Same reality, but all *different ways of perceiving it. The choice is firmly up to you. You are feeling increasingly alive as you witness and experience the changes around you. Your Light will grow ever brighter and will create higher expressions of self, as you grow your aliveness. Does this thought make your cells tingle with excitement? You have been waiting for this experience so that you can finally come alive, really alive, like never before. When you do so, you affect others; it's contagious, while unspoken. Whatever positive changes you grow within you are truly gifts to others. So know that you are serving the greater good when you come alive on your own. You are always in service, unseen. It can serve in both "positive" and "negative" ways. But as you continue on this path of evolution, the positive influences greatly outweigh those influences that hold the collective back. Be easy on yourselves; you are all in this together. Do not chide or treat yourself with anything but respect. These are difficult times. Just do your best and when you fall off the wagon, simply get back on, unscathed.*

Hilarion

I wish to lead you through a very simple exercise, but one that will prove meaningful and powerful. You can even call on me and I will be with you as you perform this technique. Read through this exercise and then... Close your eyes and put your focus on your beautiful heart. Tune into your very heart beat which keeps you alive, and then connect to the heart at the very core of your very earth. Even if you can't feel your heart beat, imagine it and hear it in your mind. And then imagine your heart beating as one with the heart at the core of the earth. Yes, match your heart's beat exactly with the earth's heart beat. Connect with earth as a living being, just like you. You are helping the earth by embracing your vital connection to it, and the earth is helping you by grounding you in your physical life. You must stay grounded no matter how "up in the clouds" you become as a result of raising your vibrations. Just keep grounding. Ideally, you can get out in nature, but this is something you can do no matter where you are and it takes only a few moments. And as you do so, feel love and gratitude for the planet that gives you life, and supports your beating heart and blessed physical existence.

Archangel Uriel

Make way for change like you have never experienced before... nothing close! I say this not to frighten you, for those of you who fear change. Rather, I wish to prepare you for great changes that are all for the highest good. You have a choice to embrace these changes, or let them paralyze you. I highly recommend you learn to embrace the new that is arriving at great speed now. Ways of living on this planet simply must change in order to provide you the opportunity to live and be sustained physically in future years. The old ways simply could not continue as they have, or you would have seen the most negative aspects of change and consequences ima-ginable. So for those who fear change, grasp this perspective and embrace the positive changes that are not only going to save this earth, but move it into a higher vibration along with its inhabitants. Be excited about the Heaven on earth that will be yours to fully experience. Bless each change, even if it means living in a different place. Or spending your time differently. Or changing your habits from third dimensional to higher ways of being. Or closing your eyes to the past. Move forward with grace.

And from our many spirit guides, so prevalent now, and helping us through...

John Lennon

Many were saddened by my passing, but know that I am doing great work here. I come through to many of you, some are aware and some are not. My message of peace on earth, above all else, is now resonating in your hearts with the promise of peace as your primary focus and goal. And it shall be, peace on your planet will come to fruition. Many things have been coming together to create this and will continue to. From your perspective, you see the tragic and horrific occurrences—from the wars and all kinds of violence to all avenues of destruction that have plagued earth for too long—which have led to the waking up of humanity. But what is key now is the collective of hearts who have long desired peace that are actually driving the change along with earth's desire. Peace will naturally exist with love as the commanding force. Insist on love, demand love, and most of all simply be love, and in these actions you will find a peace unlike that you have never experienced before. Peace will reign and you can start to know just what that will feel like, now.

Michael Jackson

You know me as a performer, a singer, and a dancer, but most of you do not know me as a soul.

This channel bravely takes a risk adding my message here because I have been judged and scorned in my earthly life and my mere presence here may put off some readers. My message has always been one of love and peace on earth. I incorporated it into my music in a way that would reach many souls, particularly those of the younger generations, to express my great love for earth and its peoples, as well as to help, in my own way, move this earth on its present course. I suffered greatly as a human, despite the gifts of fame and fortune; my suffering was so much greater. I am free now and have been in communication with many souls, helping them to feel love, not fear, and grow their connection with other dimensions. Even though you do not see me, and even though my music still has impact, my presence in this way is serving in greater ways, albeit unseen to most human beings. I share this for so many reasons. One is to give comfort to those who have lost loved ones, in a physical sense. We still go on as always, and, truly, in much grander ways.

Carl Jung

My crowning personal achievement, the discovery of synchronicity, is now being understood like never before. It is being recognized for the magical force and supreme creative tool that it is. As the veils continue to thin, and this force naturally grows in strength, it will become so commonplace and so understood, that it will simply be as much a part of life as taking your every breath. These are not just words, I mean them sincerely. Synchronicity will be incorporated into your ways of being in the world. It will outshine many of the things you have valued in the past, and you will see it as the constant gift that it is. It will become a natural part of life, as it already has become for some seekers. And for those of you who get frustrated when you cannot read the signs, I assure you that signs will not be confusing in the higher vibrations. They will not only be more obvious, but you will have a much greater, inherent understanding of things. You will sense and know things like never before. And synchronicity will beautifully work in tandem with your growing telepathic and intuitive understandings. It will be a beautiful dance.

Indira Gandhi

This channel is surprised that I am coming through, for she doesn't really know anything about me as a former leader in India, and she at first thought I was Mahatma Gandhi. But it is me, Indira Gandhi, former prime minister of India, and I have an important message. Forgive your leaders, your past political leaders, all those who have had tremendous responsibilities and power and in many ways led this world further from love, rather than toward it. As you read these words, specific names will come to mind, perhaps mine among them. It may even bring up anger and your body may tense, and that is not my intention, although it may be a necessary step in the process of letting go of the past, in this way, as well. Forgive our mistakes, often horrific mistakes. Forgive our straying from God's will and rather enforcing our own will, or the will of those with lower vibrations that have wreaked havoc on countless lives as well as the earth herself. Both individual and collective energies created karma that plague not only people, but regions, countries, and all that is. As you move toward peace on this planet, this karma will be released. You can help this process through your forgiveness and higher understanding. One day, these will be distant memories and a very old and obsolete history, because you will be in a very new existence. So let go and let God. Be well and free.

Walt Disney

My mission on earth, ultimately, was to bring joy, primarily to children, but to all through the eyes of children. To entertain, delight, and put smiles on the faces of those embracing the innocence and utter joy of living. This is still my passion and focus. Many of us send messages of embracing the child in you, and this message is more profound now than ever. You are entering times of such wonder, magic, and miracles. See the new, evolving ways of the world as a child would. Embrace the wonder. Imagine the possibilities. Feel the joy of higher living. Laugh with utter abandon and release yourself from the pain and struggles that are leaving with your third dimensional existence. You are starting anew, like a child in a whole new life, except your reincarnation is not necessary!

Albert Einstein

I am among many of you, working with you to grow your connection to God, the science of God that is far from being truly understood. One of my greatest understandings as a scientist was that when I connected through the wisdom of my heart, my most profound teachings came forth and with the greatest of ease. The connection with your heart is your most important relationship, as you connect with who you are and the part of God that resides in you. This is a magical connection that you are learning to embrace. As you delve deeper into your heart, you will find a peace that is unattainable outside of you. This means that you can be at peace no matter what is occurring around you. Do you understand the significance of this relationship? To think that your greatest gift lies right within you, and you simply need to go within and receive the endless flow of true abundance, true wealth, and true faith realized.

Emily Dickenson

The written as well as spoken word are what you primarily use to communicate. It is an art practiced not just by those who write or wrote as a profession, but by every human being. To speak or write is a fine art indeed, for you have the freedom and endless choice of words to communicate your thoughts and feelings. Our words have been our best vehicle for communication. However, this is changing, and changing rapidly. There is a better way to express oneself completely. Words can fall short. But words combined with feelings, temperament, color, sound, vibration—all the energy that goes into a thought or feeling—are, cumulatively, a much grander expression. And this is the gift of moving into telepathic communications. When you converse telepathically, it will express a poetry that mere words never could. You are evolving into a time of grand and full expression of the poetic nature of your very souls.

Lucille Ball

I assure you that this channel is not off her rocker! Channeling Lucy? She and her friend have seen my face in the clouds and she is not totally surprised that I'm coming through. She is feeling excited about all of us coming through to her, but she also knows that she will be judged and some people may roll their eyes when they read these messages. Could this really be? Can you all really connect with us? Well let me tell you, I have worked with many on earth, helping them in ways that I can best serve. So this is really nothing new. However, not all receivers are consciously aware that it is actually me. They may just hear my whispers but not understand the source. You are being challenged to not just entertain this idea, for those this is new to, but also to get used to this kind of connection to the "other side." However, it isn't always going to feel like the "other side." We are growing closer and closer. This channel's work is preparing you to get much more comfortable with the idea of accessing guidance and wisdom from those who have a high perspective on things. When it comes to me, of course you think of comedy and making people laugh. Yes, I was a million laughs. It wasn't until I transitioned that I realized what my work was truly about. I was a healer without really knowing it. I worked my way to the top to entertain, but, actually, I was helping people to heal and cope in life through the energy of laughter.

A final message from Michael and Mary

Thank you for reading this book. You are to be commended for actively pursuing the understanding and embracing of the new ways of being, as you are each a vital part of bringing Heaven onto earth. We all join together in celebration over just how far you have come. We celebrate your courage. We celebrate your determination and relentless faith. We celebrate what you may deem as your each and every "success" and "failure," as they all brought the whole to this very point in time... a time of great change and creation of a whole new era.

In a way, your work is just beginning, and yet the hardest work is done. That may appear contradictory, so let us explain further. You have passed through a portal of change, a new realignment, that will make everything much easier. There is much to do, so many changes that will occur. However, the pressure is off now, as a great deal has been cleared. If you are reading this book, you are likely among the forerunners who have or are in the process of releasing your past completely. This has been the hardest work: working on the self while also dealing with your changing bodies, and a new relationship of your body to the earth and all that is. Very difficult. You have succeeded and actually completed much of the personal birthing process, as described.

Now comes the work to rebuild this world. Things will fall and things will need to be "cleaned up." And then there is the building of the new. Every aspect of life will be recreated with you, the creative pioneers, utilizing the new energy to define and determine these changes in: politics, food, media, entertainment, business, money, products, and our relationships to each other, animals, plants, and the environment—to name just a few. Truly, no aspect of life will go untouched during this process!

Even with so much work to be done, in these higher vibrations there will be greater support and growing ease for change. There is also building excitement knowing that better times are on the horizon. Since the 12/21/12 date, a darkness that held the energy of fear has been released and transmuted. That alone has taken much weight off of your collective shoulders so that you can move forward with more ease.

Take a moment to celebrate yourself for your grand accomplishments, knowing that you will be rewarded over time in ways that will astound you. One day, you will look back and say, "This was all worth it, more than worth it!" For you are part of changing this world and the Universe forevermore. Could there be anything grander? Could there be anything more fulfilling for a human being? And when you unite with your soul, while living in a physical body, you will then define the love that you truly are.

Look up, look up to the sky, feel the sun on your face, and know that your connection to the sun, the New Sun beyond your sun, is providing a new path to an enlightenment you have never known. Embrace this understanding and celebrate the unknown. Grow a conscious relationship to the New Sun, right from your heart. See what develops; the understandings, feelings, and, yes, the physical changes in you as you increasingly receive this most precious gift of Liquid Light. As your quest for the material continues to lose importance, and the desire for what is truly real and life-sustaining grows, your capacity for joy bursts into new territory.

ABOUT THE AUTHOR

Mary Soliel is an author, visionary, spiritual teacher, and self-described "synchronist." Her three-time award-winning book, *I Can See Clearly Now: How Synchronicity Illuminates Our Lives,* is a groundbreaking exploration of the phenomenon of synchronicity.

As a channel of Archangel Michael, the publishing of *Michael's Clarion Call: Messages from the Archangel for Creating Heaven on Earth,* and now *The New Sun,* highlights Mary's mission as a teacher and messenger to globally raise awareness of the Golden Age before us. She is available for U.S. and international speaking engagements and workshops, and radio/print/television interviews. Visit her at: www.marysoliel.com.